HBJ SPELLING

GREEN

Richard Madden

Thorsten Carlson

Harcourt Brace Jovanovich, Publishers

Orlando   New York   Chicago   San Diego   Atlanta   Dallas

Acknowledgments

ACKNOWLEDGMENT

Handwriting models in this book are reproduced with permission of Zaner-Bloser, Inc., from the series *Creative Growth with Handwriting,* © 1975, 1979.

ART CREDITS

Yvette Banek: 29, 34, 40, 49 (b), 70, 74, 101, 118, 130, 138, 145; Kevin Callahan: 20, 27, 41, 48, 49 (t), 59, 66, 71, 88, 89, 91, 98, 103, 107, 125, 136, 137 (t); Tom Cooke: 4, 5, 6, 22, 23, 26, 32 (b), 44, 46 (b), 56 (b), 58, 64 (t), 65, 78, 80, 94, 100 (t), 108, 123, 140; Len Ebert: 13, 32 (t), 45, 56, 61 (t), 76, 105, 110, 129 (b), 143, 146; Arthur Friedman: 16, 18, 62, 72, 79, 99 (b), 102, 122; John Killgrew: 7, 24, 25, 38, 53, 60, 63, 77, 92 (b), 104 (t), 132; Jared Lee: 8, 35, 61 (b), 96, 109, 116, 117 (b), 119, 128, 133, 139; Sal Murdocca: 10, 17, 21, 47, 57, 68, 75, 84, 104 (b), 117 (t), 124, 137 (b), 141, 144; Blanche Sims: 9, 12, 33, 37, 39, 51, 64 (b), 69, 82, 85, 100 (b), 115, 120; Jenny Williams: 15, 28, 36, 46 (t), 52, 67, 83, 92 (t), 99 (t), 112, 129 (t), 131, 142 (b).
KEY: top (t); bottom (b); left (l); right (r); center (c).

PHOTO CREDITS

Cover, © Phoebe Dunn/DPI; pages 13, © HBJ Studio; 31, © The Granger Collection; 37, © Carole Feuerberg; 52, © Ken Lax/The Stock Shop; 55, © Randa Bishop/DPI; 68, © ZEFA/H. Armstrong Roberts; 73, © H. Armstrong Roberts; 81, © Phoebe Dunn/DPI; 86, © Eric Carle/Shostal Associates; 89, © Courtesy of American Telephone and Telegraph Company; 90, © Shostal Associates; 93, © Stan Wayman/Photo Researchers; 97 (l), © G. Trouillet/ The Image Bank; 97 (c), © Rhoda Galyn; 97 (r), © Runk/Schoenberger/Grant Heilman; 111 (t-l), © H. Armstrong Roberts; 111 (b-l), © Wildlife Unlimited/Tom McHugh/NAS-PR.; 111 (b-r), © Walter Chandoha; 113, © HBJ Studio; 114, © Mimi Forsyth/Monkmeyer Press Photo; 121, © Eric Arnesen/HBJ Photo; 126, © H. Armstrong Roberts; 134, © Ruth Dixon; 147, © Juergen Schmitt/DPI; 149, © J. H. Robinson/Photo Researchers; 150, © Hans Reinhard/ Bruce Coleman; 153, © Pat Myers; 155, © Antonio Mendoza/Stock, Boston; 157, © Stephen Krasemann/Photo Researchers; 159, © Leonard Lee Rue III/Photo Researchers; 160, © M. J. Germana/DPI; 161, © George Roos/ DPI; 163, © Kim Massie/Rainbow; 165, © Tana Hoban/DPI; 167, © G. Schaller/Bruce Coleman; 168, © Walter Chandoha; 170, © Joe McDonald/Bruce Coleman; 172, © A. B. Joyce/Photo Researchers; 174, © Phil Dotson/ DPI; 176, © H. Armstrong Roberts; 177, © Paul Kuhn/Bruce Coleman; 179, © Hans Pfletschinger/Peter Arnold; 180, © HBJ Photo; 183, © E. Bordis/De Wys; 184, © George Holton/Photo Researchers; 185, © Joe McDonald/ Bruce Coleman; 186, © Mira Atkeson/DPI; 188, © Irene Vandermolen/Bruce Coleman.

Contents

Skills Check

A. Write a word you know that has each vowel sound.

1. short a̲
2. short e̲
3. short i̲
4. short o̲
5. short u̲

6. long a̲
7. long e̲
8. long i̲
9. long o̲

B. Add beginning letters. Use different letters to write two different words each time.

10. _ op
11. _ an
12. _ ame
13. _ ee
14. _ ide
15. _ ut

C. Two words in each row rhyme. One does not. Write the word that does not rhyme.

16. gave   have   save
17. near   hear   bear
18. hair   there   were
19. what   that   cat

D. Write each list of words in ABC order.

20. please   **21.** why
     paint   your
     neck   winter
     made   wrong

E. Write the words that mean the opposite.

22. up   **23.** left   **24.** on
25. before   **26.** in   **27.** stop

F. Write an "action word" to finish each sentence.

28. Robin will ____ us a story.
29. Dennis will ____ dinner with us.
30. Tammy will ____ her bike to school.
31. Brian will ____ the game with us.
32. Wendy will ____ in the pool.

G. Say each word. Write a word that sounds the same but is not spelled the same.

33. wood   **34.** there
35. hear   **36.** rode
37. right   **38.** no
39. blew   **40.** deer

3

1 Short Vowel Sounds

1. flag
2. fed
3. hid
4. dot
5. hunt
6. apple
7. bring
8. club
9. else
10. happy
11. pen
12. river
13. rock
14. shall
15. sunny

This Week's Words

All of this week's words have short vowel sounds. These are the signs for the short vowel sounds.

/a/   /e/   /i/   /o/   /u/

These sounds are usually spelled with one vowel letter.

You hear all the short vowel sounds in this sentence:

/a/ /e/ /i/ /o/ /u/
Fat hens will not run.

Remember this sentence. It will help you to remember which sounds are spelled with only one vowel letter.

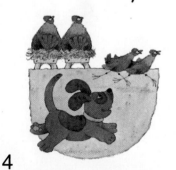

4

Spelling Practice

flag
fed
hid
dot
hunt
apple
bring
club
else
happy
pen
river
rock
shall
sunny

A. Finish the sentences. Use this week's words.

1. The vowel sound /a/ is spelled with ＿＿ in fat, ＿＿, ＿＿, ＿＿, and ＿＿.

2. The vowel sound /e/ is spelled with ＿＿ in hens, ＿＿, ＿＿, and ＿＿.

3. The vowel sound /i/ is spelled with ＿＿ in will, ＿＿, ＿＿, and ＿＿.

4. The vowel sound /o/ is spelled with ＿＿ in not, ＿＿, and ＿＿.

5. The vowel sound /u/ is spelled with ＿＿ in run, ＿＿, ＿＿, and ＿＿.

B. Write the words that start with the same sounds as the picture names.

6.

7.

C. Write the words that end with the same sounds as the picture names.

8.

9.

5

Spelling and Language

flag
fed
hid
dot
hunt
apple
bring
club
else
happy
pen
river
rock
shall
sunny

PLURALS

A **plural** names more than one. Add <u>s</u> to make most words plurals.

hen   **hens**

Finish the sentences. Use the plurals of some of this week's words.

1. Do you have enough ___ to make a pie?
2. Craig has lots of pencils and ___.
3. Pete and I belong to different book ___.
4. Katie likes to fish in ___ and streams.
5. Tina drew lines between the ___ and solved the picture puzzle.
6. We all carried ___ in the big parade.
7. Stones are smaller and smoother than ___.

HANDWRITING

i I   t T   l L   e E

The letters **i, t, l,** and **e** begin with this stroke. ___

1. Practice writing **i l, t T, l L, e E** in cursive.
2. Write this sentence: *I let Eli tell it.*

6

Spelling Review

Words can make you think of other words. For example, leap might make you think frog. And quiet as a might make you think mouse. Write this week's words to go with these words.

1. treasure ___
2. ___ and ink
3. join the ___
4. ___ the i
5. bright and ___
6. anything ___
7. ___ it here
8. ___ ending
9. cross the ___
10. ___ or will
11. ___ the dog
12. ___ pie
13. hard as a ___
14. wave a ___
15. ran and ___

MASTERY WORDS

Follow the directions. Use the Mastery words.
1. Write the two words that begin with a vowel letter.
2. Write the two words that have short a.

Write the Mastery word that rhymes with each word.
3. beg   4. hit   5. hop   6. fast

and
last
leg
sit
top
until

BONUS WORDS

Add the missing letters and write Bonus words.
1. ___ift   2. ___ock   3. ___elt   4. ___ash
5. ___ap   6. ___op   7. ___uck   8. ___ell

Now add different beginning consonant letters to the word parts above. For example, you can add l to ift to make lift or dr to make drift. See how many different words you can make.

struck
smash
dwell
melt
flock
crop
strap
swift

7

2 Double Letters

1. spill
2. drill
3. ill
4. shell
5. spell
6. smell
7. stuff
8. cliff
9. kiss
10. less
11. mess
12. unless
13. add
14. odd
15. roll

This Week's Words

Most of this week's words have a short vowel sound. Most of them end with the consonant sound /l/, /f/, or /s/. These consonant sounds are spelled with two consonant letters.

- /l/ is spelled **ll** in spill
- /f/ is spelled **ff** in stuff
- /s/ is spelled **ss** in kiss

Double consonant letters also spell /d/ in add and odd.

☐ The word roll does not have a short vowel sound. What vowel sound do you hear in roll?

REMEMBER THIS:

One d is enough for bad and sad
And lad and had and even mad.
But when it comes to spelling add,
Another d you'll have to add.

One d will do for cod and nod,
And one's enough for rod and pod.
But odd is odd, as you can see,
It needs a second letter d.

8

Spelling Practice

A. Follow the directions. Use this week's words.

1. Write the six words that have the vowel sound /e/.

2. Write the five words that have the vowel sound /i/.

3. Write the word that has a long <u>o</u>.

4. Write the word that rhymes with <u>nod</u>.

5. Write the word that rhymes with <u>sad</u>.

B. Finish the story with this week's words. The consonant sound that ends the word is given to help you. This will help you get started. The answer for **6** is <u>mess</u>.

My room is a __6__ /s/. Dad says I can't go to Ben's party __7__ /s/ I clean my room today. He's right. But cleaning my room makes me feel __8__ /l/. There is so much __9__ /f/ to put away. Here is the __10__ /d/ little __11__ /l/ I found on the beach. I could __12__ /l/ a hole in it and wear it on a chain. But it has a funny __13__ /l/. I guess I should throw it away.

spill
drill
ill
shell
spell
smell
stuff
cliff
kiss
less
mess
unless
add
odd
roll

9

spill
drill
ill
shell
spell
smell
stuff
cliff
kiss
less
mess
unless
add
odd
roll

Spelling and Language

WORD LADDERS

Changing one letter can make a different word. Take <u>add</u>. Write <u>o</u> in place of <u>a</u>, and you spell <u>odd</u>. Start with the words below. Change a letter. The new letter is the first letter in the picture word. The ▲ shows where the new letter goes.

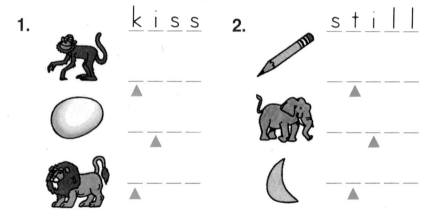

1. k i s s   2.   s t i l l

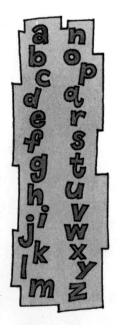

The Dictionary

The words in a dictionary are in alphabetical order. **Alphabetical order** is the order of letters from <u>a</u> to <u>z</u>. <u>A</u>pple, <u>b</u>ring, <u>c</u>lub are in alphabetical order by first letter—<u>a</u>, <u>b</u>, <u>c</u>. A<u>b</u>le, a<u>c</u>t, a<u>d</u>d are in alphabetical order by second letter—<u>b</u>, <u>c</u>, <u>d</u>.

Write these groups of words in alphabetical order.

1. cliff
   ill
   add
   roll

2. spell
   stuff
   shell
   smell

Spelling Review

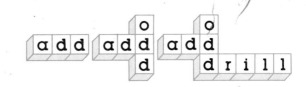

THIS WEEK'S WORDS

Make a "word chain" with this week's words. Write one word. Use a letter in that word to write another word. Then keep going, writing words across and down. Try to link up all the words in one chain. Or you may make more than one chain.

MASTERY WORDS

Follow the directions. Use the Mastery words.
1. Write the two words that begin with two consonant letters.
2. Write the two words that begin with a vowel letter.

Write the Mastery word that rhymes with each word below.

3. well   **4.** hill   **5.** pass   **6.** full

Write the Mastery words that go with these words.
7. on and _____   **8.** chicken and _____

egg
fell
grass
off
pull
still

BONUS WORDS

Write the Bonus word that goes with each meaning.
1. play period   **2.** place to rest your head
3. creamy dessert   **4.** without warning
5. small town   **6.** place between mountains
7. full of mist
8. marks of very old plants and animals

Write a short story. Try to use all the Bonus words.

foggy
fossils
pillow
pudding
recess
sudden
valley
village

3 Using Verbs

1. bat
2. chop
3. clap
4. drop
5. nap
6. pin
7. step
8. skinned
9. stopped
10. trapped
11. tripped
12. tagging
13. planning
14. wagging
15. tapping

The dogs <u>wag</u> their tails.

This Week's Words

The word <u>wag</u> is a **verb,** or "action word." It ends with one vowel letter and one consonant letter. You can add <u>ed</u> to <u>wag</u> to make a word that tells about the past. When you add <u>ed</u>, you must double the last letter.

The dogs <u>wagged</u> their tails.

You can also add <u>ing</u> to <u>wag</u>. When you add <u>ing</u>, you must also double the last letter.

The dogs were <u>wagging</u> their tails.

All of this week's words are verbs. They all follow this pattern.

wag   wagged   wagging

Spelling Practice

bat
chop
clap
drop
nap
pin
step
skinned
stopped
trapped
tripped
tagging
planning
wagging
tapping

A. Write the verbs that go with the pictures. Use this week's words.

1.   **2.**   **3.**

B. Add <u>ed</u> to each of these words.

4. trip   **5.** skin   **6.** stop   **7.** trap

C. Add <u>ing</u> to each of these words.

8. wag   **9.** plan   **10.** tap   **11.** tag

D. Finish the sentences. Use this week's words.

12. We ___ to show we enjoy something.
13. Don't ___ in the wet cement!
14. Chee will ___ the letters in the mailbox.
15. Alex helped Dad ___ wood for the fire.

E. Try this "word math."

16. stopped − ed = ___ + ing = ___
17. planning − ing = ___ + ed = ___
18. tripped − ed = ___ + ing = ___

bat
chop
clap
drop
nap
pin
step
skinned
stopped
trapped
tripped
tagging
planning
wagging
tapping

Spelling and Language

ADDING ed AND ing

You add <u>ed</u> to a word to tell what already happened. You add <u>ing</u> to make a word that can be used with such words as <u>am</u>, <u>is</u>, <u>are</u>, <u>was</u>, and <u>were</u>.

Add <u>ed</u> to the word in dark print. Finish the sentence.

1. **clap**   We ___ until our hands were red.
2. **pin**   Tom ___ a note on the pillow.
3. **bat**   The cat ___ the toy mouse under the bed.

Add <u>ing</u> to the word in dark print. Finish the sentence.

4. **nap**   Nell was ___ when I called.
5. **chop**   Alice is ___ mushrooms for the pizza.
6. **tag**   Sam's dog was ___ along after us.

HANDWRITING

r R   s S   p P

r   s   p

Notice where the beginning stroke stops in each letter.

1. Practice writing **r R, s S, p P** in cursive.

2. Write this sentence: *Peter sells pies.*

Spelling Review

bat

bat

THIS WEEK'S WORDS

All of these words are **verbs.** But they can also be used as **nouns,** or "naming words." <u>Bat</u> is a verb when you say "<u>Bat</u> the ball." But it is a noun when you say "Use my <u>bat</u>."

Write sentences using this week's words as nouns. You will have to take <u>ed</u> and <u>ing</u> off such words as skinned and planning.

MASTERY WORDS

Follow the directions. Use the Mastery words.
1. Write the three words that begin like <u>paw</u>.
2. Write the three words that end like <u>cat</u>.

Finish each sentence pair. Use a Mastery word.
3. Rabbits are hopping. Rabbits ____.
4. I am petting the dog. I ____ the dog.
5. Balloons are popping. Balloons ____.
6. I am rubbing my eyes. I ____ my eyes.

> hop
> pat
> rub
> pet
> spot
> pop

BONUS WORDS

Write the Bonus word that rhymes with each word.
1. clapping   2. club   3. purring   4. hot

Follow the directions. Use the Bonus words.
5. Write the word that rhymes with <u>pop</u> but isn't spelled with <u>o</u>.
6. Add <u>ed</u> to each word. Two already have <u>ed</u>. You will have to take <u>ing</u> off two words and add <u>ed</u>. Then use each word in a sentence.

> scrub
> swap
> prop
> plot
> grabbed
> shopped
> wrapping
> stirring

15

4 Consonant Clusters

1. clear
2. close
3. drawer
4. drive
5. flat
6. floor
7. print
8. snow
9. star
10. state
11. stick
12. trick
13. string
14. spray
15. spring

This Week's Words

Say the word <u>clear</u> to yourself. You hear two consonant sounds at the beginning of <u>clear</u> — /k/ and /l/. These sounds are spelled with **c** and **l**.

The letters **cl** in <u>clear</u> are called a **consonant cluster.** The letters are written together. You hear the sounds of the letters together.

Sometimes three consonant letters make up a consonant cluster. The letters **spr** in <u>spray</u> are a consonant cluster. You hear all three consonant sounds at the beginning of <u>spray</u>.

REMEMBER THIS: The word <u>close</u> can be said two ways. You say it one way when you say "<u>Close</u> your eyes." You say it another way when you say "Stand <u>close</u> to the table." But either way you say it, it is spelled the same: <u>close</u>.

16

Spelling Practice

A. Follow the directions. Use this week's words.

1. Write the four words that have <u>l</u> in the consonant cluster.

2. Write the seven words that have <u>r</u> in the consonant cluster.

3. Write the three words that begin with the same cluster as <u>stop</u>.

4. Write the three words that have a three-letter cluster.

5. Write the word that ends with <u>er</u>.

B. Finish the story with this week's words. The consonant clusters in ( ) will help you.

Jake was cold. He got up to (cl) __6__ the window. The (fl) __7__ felt icy under his feet. He looked out. There was fresh (sn) __8__ on the ground. The sky was (cl) __9__. He saw a falling (st) __10__. It made a (str) __11__ of light in the sky.

clear
close
drawer
drive
flat
floor
print
snow
star
state
stick
trick
string
spray
spring

Spelling and Language

clear
close
drawer
drive
flat
floor
print
snow
star
state
stick
trick
string
spray
spring

NOUNS AND VERBS

A **noun** names a person, a place, or a thing. A **verb** shows action or being. Finish each pair of sentences with one of this week's words. The word will be a verb in the first sentence and a noun in the second.

1. Tomorrow we will ____ to the mountains.
2. It is a beautiful ____ in the fall.
3. Let's ____ Mimi into thinking we're not here.
4. Mimi will laugh about our ____.
5. Don't ____ your foot out of the boat!
6. Use a ____ to see how deep the water is.

The Dictionary

On a dictionary page, an **entry word** is a word in dark print. The meanings of the entry words are given. All entry words appear in alphabetical order.

> ►**bus·y** /biz′ē/ *adj.* **1** Doing things: I'm *busy* making lunch. **2** Full of things to do: I had a *busy* day.
> ►**but·ter** /but′ər/ *n.* A yellow spread for bread made from cream. —*v.* To spread butter on.
> ►**but·ter·fly** /but′ər·flī′/ *n., pl.* **butterflies** An insect with four bright-colored wings.

Look up each word below in the spelling dictionary. Then write the entry word that follows it.

1. start
2. princess
3. draw
4. spread
5. spot
6. sneeze

18

Spelling Review

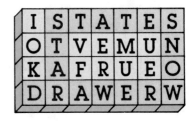

THIS WEEK'S WORDS

Use all the words to make a word search puzzle. You can write the words across or down. Fill in the empty spaces with other letters. Then let someone else solve it.

MASTERY WORDS

Write the Mastery word that begins with the same two letters as each word.

1. smile   **2.** free   **3.** sweet   **4.** glass

Write Mastery words that mean the opposite.

5. stop   **6.** go   **7.** large   **8.** sad

Put the words in order and write two sentences.

9. from   beginning.   Start   the
10. stay   some   Let's   and   swim   more.

> **from**
> **glad**
> **small**
> **start**
> **stay**
> **swim**

BONUS WORDS

1. Combine the beginning consonant clusters at the left with the word endings at the right. Spell as many different words as you can.

spr	scr	sp
pl	fr	bl
	fl	spl

ead	atch
ace	ame
ast	ash	it

2. Write the Bonus word you could not spell in **1.**
3. Write a story about outer space. Use all the Bonus words.

> **blast**
> **flash**
> **frame**
> **planet**
> **scratch**
> **space**
> **split**
> **spread**

19

5 More Consonant Clusters

1. act
2. dust
3. east
4. test
5. west
6. lift
7. bend
8. grand
9. ground
10. wind
11. build
12. child
13. wild
14. milk
15. bump

This Week's Words

The letters **cl** in <u>clear</u> are called a consonant cluster. Consonant clusters do not always come at the beginning of words. Often they come at the end of words.

Say the word <u>act</u> to yourself. Listen carefully for the consonant sounds /k/ and /t/ at the end of <u>act</u>. The letters **ct** in <u>act</u> are a consonant cluster.

REMEMBER THIS: The vowel sound /i/ in <u>build</u> is spelled <u>ui</u>. Here is the reason why. Hundreds of years ago, the word was sometimes spelled with <u>u</u>, <u>buld</u>, and sometimes spelled with <u>i</u>, <u>bild</u>. No one could decide which was right—<u>u</u> or <u>i</u>. So they decided to use them both!

I spell it with **i**. You spell it with **u**. Then **you** and **I** will spell it with **ui**!

Spelling Practice

A. Follow the directions. Use this week's words.

1. Write the two words that begin with the same consonant cluster and end with the same cluster.

2. Write the three words that end with <u>ld</u>.

B. Write the word that rhymes with each word.

3. jump

4. drift

5. fact

6. silk

C. Finish the sentences. Use this week's words.

7. I forgot to ___ my watch.

8. The ___ blew the leaves around.
   Circle the word you wrote that rhymes with <u>kind</u>.

D. Write the words that end with the same cluster as the picture word does.

band

last

9.

10.

act
dust
east
test
west
lift
bend
grand
ground
wind
build
child
wild
milk
bump

21

Spelling and Language

act
dust
east
test
west
lift
bend
grand
ground
wind
build
child
wild
milk
bump

TALKING ABOUT THE PAST

You just add <u>ed</u> to most verbs to tell what already happened. Write these sentences over. Add <u>ed</u> to the underlined words. Make the sentences tell about the past.

1. Strong winds <u>lift</u> the car off the ground.
2. The man and the child <u>milk</u> the cows.
3. Carlos and Hilda <u>dust</u> the grand piano.
4. I <u>act</u> wild when I <u>bump</u> my funny bone.

HANDWRITING

h H k K b B f F

The letters **h**, **k**, **b**, and **f** all begin with the same stroke.

1. Practice writing **h H, k K, b B, f F** in cursive.

2. Write this sentence:

   Help Beth lift her bike.

Spelling Review

THIS WEEK'S WORDS

Change the underlined letter in each word.
Write one of this week's words.

1. b<u>a</u>nd
2. buil<u>t</u>
3. li<u>s</u>t
4. dus<u>k</u>
5. a<u>n</u>t
6. te<u>n</u>t
7. gran<u>t</u>
8. win<u>k</u>
9. we<u>n</u>t
10. <u>m</u>ild
11. <u>h</u>ump
12. <u>a</u>round
13. eas<u>y</u>
14. mil<u>l</u>

Use the word you haven't written yet in a sentence.

MASTERY WORDS

1. Write the three Mastery words that have <u>t</u> in the consonant cluster.
2. Write the two words that have <u>d</u> in the consonant cluster.
3. Write the three words that have short <u>e</u>.
4. Add <u>ed</u> to <u>help</u>. Use the word in a sentence.

felt
hand
help
hold
left
want

BONUS WORDS

1. Write the four Bonus words that begin and end with consonant clusters.
2. Write the three words that each have two vowel sounds.
3. Write the word that rhymes with <u>first</u> and <u>worst</u>.
4. The words <u>stamp</u> and <u>tramp</u> both end with <u>amp</u>. Add different consonants to <u>amp</u>. Spell as many words as you can. Then do the same thing with <u>end</u> in <u>blend</u>.

adult
blend
burst
insect
prompt
pumpkin
stamp
tramp

23

6 More Letters Than Sounds

1. another
2. together
3. weather
4. chin
5. reach
6. which
7. teacher
8. catch
9. kitchen
10. shine
11. shout
12. crash
13. strong
14. angry
15. hungry

That child should sing.

This Week's Words

The words this week have consonant sounds that are spelled with more than one letter. You hear those sounds in this sentence.

/th/ /ch/ /sh/   /ng/
That child should sing.

● The first sound in <u>that</u> is spelled **th.**
    ano<u>th</u>er

● The first sound in <u>child</u> is spelled **ch** or **tch.**
    <u>ch</u>in   rea<u>ch</u>   ca<u>tch</u>

● The first sound in <u>should</u> is spelled **sh.**
    <u>sh</u>ine   cra<u>sh</u>

● The last sound in <u>sing</u> is spelled **ng** or **n.**
    stro<u>ng</u>   a<u>n</u>gry

Spelling Practice

A. Finish the sentences. Use this week's words that have /ch/.

1. Everyone in my class likes our ___.
2. Are you tall enough to ___ the top shelf?
3. Kenny is in the ___ helping with dinner.
4. Tell me ___ book you like best.
5. Frogs ___ flies with their tongues.
6. Ming cut her ___ when she fell.

B. Draw a line under the letters that spell /ch/ in the six words you just wrote.

C. Now follow these directions. Use this week's words.

7. Write the two words that begin with consonant clusters.
8. Write the four words that end with <u>er</u>. Then draw a line under the two consonant letters that stand for one sound.
9. Write the two words that end with long <u>e</u> sounds.
10. Write the word that sounds like <u>witch</u>.

D. Write the words that go with these words. Use words that start with /sh/.

11. Don't ___!   **12.** Rise and ___!

another
together
weather
chin
reach
which
teacher
catch
kitchen
shine
shout
crash
strong
angry
hungry

another
together
weather
chin
reach
which
teacher
catch
kitchen
shine
shout
crash
strong
angry
hungry

Spelling and Language

WRITING SENTENCES

Put the words in order and write four sentences. Remember that a sentence starts with a capital letter and ends with a period.

1. kitchen went for I the sandwich. to a
2. peanut could the butter. reach I not
3. crashed the The floor. jar on
4. before could It catch fell I it.

The Dictionary

There are two **guide words** at the top of each dictionary page. The word on the left is the first word on the page. The word on the right is the last word. All the other words on the page are in alphabetical order between the guide words.

ear	everyone
ear¹ /ir/ *n.* What people and animals use for hearing. **ear²** /ir/ *n.* Where grain grows on some plants: an *ear* of corn.	—*v.* **emptied, emptying** To make empty: Ben *emptied* his pockets. **en·e·my** /en′ə·mē/ *n., pl.* **enemies** A person who tries to harm another,

Pretend that these are pairs of guide words. Write two of this week's words that would be on each page.

1. all   apple
2. cent   day
3. house   knee
4. table   truck

Spelling Review

THIS WEEK'S WORDS

Letters that spell consonant sounds are missing from each word. Write the missing letters. Then write the whole word.

1. stro___
2. whi___
3. toge___er
4. cra___
5. ___ine
6. rea___
7. hu___gry
8. ki___en
9. ___out
10. a___gry
11. ___in
12. wea___er
13. ano___er
14. tea___er
15. ca___

MASTERY WORDS

Follow the directions. Use the Mastery words.
1. Write the two words that end with /ch/.
2. Write two words. One ends the way the other begins.

Write a Mastery word to go with each word.
3. open and ___
4. ___ and dinner
5. ___ and pull
6. mother and ___
7. ___ and dance
8. ___ and every

> father
> each
> lunch
> shut
> push
> sing

BONUS WORDS

1. Write the Bonus word that sounds like <u>weather</u>.
2. Write the two words that rhyme.
3. Write the two words that begin with a consonant cluster.
4. Write the word that can name someone who throws a ball or something that holds milk. Write a sentence that uses both meanings.
5. Write sentences using all the Bonus words.

> clothing
> fresh
> gather
> pitcher
> porch
> rather
> shack
> whether

7 Plurals

1. paths
2. desks
3. lists
4. fingers
5. robins
6. pictures
7. uncles
8. circuses
9. guesses
10. classes
11. bushes
12. churches
13. inches
14. ranches
15. beaches

paths

path

This Week's Words

A word that names just one thing is **singular.** A word that names more than one thing is **plural.** Here are two ways to make a word plural.

1. Add <u>s</u> to most words.

    path   paths

2. Add <u>es</u> to the words that end with <u>s</u>, <u>ss</u>, <u>sh</u>, or <u>ch</u>.

circus	circuses
class	classes
bush	bushes
beach	beaches

REMEMBER THIS: Say <u>beach</u>. Now say <u>beaches</u>. Listen to the extra vowel sound before the <u>s</u> in <u>beaches</u>. That extra vowel sound tells you to add <u>es</u>. But this doesn't work with a word like <u>faces</u>. The <u>e</u> is already there in <u>face</u>.

28

Spelling Practice

A. Write the plural of each word.

1. church
2. beach
3. inch
4. ranch

B. Write the singular for each of these words.

5. guesses
6. classes

C. Write the plural of each word in dark print and finish the sentences.

7. **robin**   I saw four ____ outside my window.
8. **uncle**   Andy has more ____ than I have.
9. **list**   Melba makes ____ of things she must do.
10. **path**   There are lots of ____ in this forest.
11. **finger**   Please don't eat with your ____!
12. **desk**   We sat at our ____ and waited.

D. Write the singular and plural words that go with the pictures.

13.   14.   15.

paths
desks
lists
fingers
robins
pictures
uncles
circuses
guesses
classes
brushes
churches
inches
ranches
beaches

paths
desks
lists
fingers
robins
pictures
uncles
circuses
guesses
classes
bushes
churches
inches
ranches
beaches

Spelling and Language

SINGULAR AND PLURAL WORDS

One of this week's words will finish each sentence. Decide if the singular or plural fits the sentence. Then write the correct one. For example, you would finish the sentence "These ___ lead into the woods" with the word paths. But you would use path in the sentence "This ___ leads into the woods."

1. Our ___ at school stand side by side.
2. That ___ has fine, white sand.
3. Be careful! Those ___ have sharp thorns.
4. How many ___ make a yard?
5. Our third-grade ___ is going to the zoo.
6. Here are some ___ Lisa took of my cat.
7. I guessed, but my ___ were all wrong.

HANDWRITING

c C   o O   a A

Join **o** to other letters at the midline.   os

Join **a** to other letters at the baseline.   as

1. Practice writing **c C, o O, a A** in cursive.
2. Practice writing **os, as, co, ca** in cursive.
3. Write this sentence: *Carlos spoke to the class.*

Spelling Review

Write sentences using all of this week's words. Try to use as many of the words as you can in each sentence. You may use the singular or the plural. Here is an example: "I have lots of <u>pictures</u> of <u>circuses</u> in my <u>desk</u>."

MASTERY WORDS

Write the plural of each word. Draw a line under the letters you added to spell the plural.

1. glass   **2.** wish   **3.** dish   **4.** duck

Finish the sentences. Use the Mastery words.

5. Please turn off the ____.
6. That dog has muddy ____.
7. Do ____ ever come true?
8. Jesse drank three ____ of milk.
9. Sara fed bread to the ____ at the pond.
10. Joan and Chet will wash the ____.

dishes
ducks
glasses
lights
paws
wishes

BONUS WORDS

1. Write the singular form of each Bonus word. Circle the singular words that end with <u>e</u>.
2. Write the names of three things you might take on a picnic.
3. Write the word for mother and father.
4. Tell about a picnic. Try to use the singular or plural of each Bonus word in your story.

bandages
branches
headaches
parents
patches
peaches
pickles
sandwiches

31

8 The Days of the Week

1. Sunday
2. Monday
3. Tuesday
4. Wednesday
5. Thursday
6. Friday
7. Saturday
8. Sun.
9. Mon.
10. Tues.
11. Wed.
12. Thurs.
13. Fri.
14. Sat.
15. week

Mon.
Tues.
Wed.
Thurs.
Fri.

Sat.

Sun.

This Week's Words

The words this week are the names of days and their abbreviations. An **abbreviation** is a short way to write a word.

The name of a day always begins with a capital letter. You need a capital to write it the short way, too. You must also put a period at the end. The period shows that you made the word shorter.

REMEMBER THIS: You don't hear the sounds of all the letters in Wednesday. Here's an idea that can help you spell it right. There are two e's in the first part. The first e is between two tall letters. The second e is between two short letters.

Wed nes

32

Spelling Practice

A. Write the full names for these abbreviations.

1. Wed. **2.** Tues.
3. Sat. **4.** Thurs.

B. Follow the directions. Use this week's words.

5. Write the names of the days that make up the weekend.

6. Write the name that rhymes with <u>Sunday</u>.

7. Write the name of a day that has a long <u>i</u> sound.

8. Write the name of a day that has "silent" letters.

9. Write the days that come before and after Wednesday.

10. Write the five abbreviations made by dropping <u>day</u>.

11. Write two abbreviations made by dropping more than <u>day</u>.

12. Finish the poem. Use one of this week's words.

> On Monday I'm quiet,
> On Tuesday I speak.
> I do something different
> Each day of the ____.

Sunday
Monday
Tuesday
Wednesday
Thursday
Friday
Saturday
Sun.
Mon.
Tues.
Wed.
Thurs.
Fri.
Sat.
week

33

Sunday
Monday
Tuesday
Wednesday
Thursday
Friday
Saturday
Sun.
Mon.
Tues.
Wed.
Thurs.
Fri.
Sat.
week

Spelling and Language

DESCRIBING WORDS

Some words describe, or tell about, other words. Happy is a describing word—happy faces. Read the sentences about Toby's week. Find a word in the box to describe each day. Write the describing word and the day.

awful	busy	noisy	perfect
rainy	strange	sunny	

1. On Sunday, it was bright and warm.
2. But on Monday, it rained all day.
3. On Tuesday, Toby had lots of things to do.
4. Wednesday was unusual. Odd things happened.
5. On Thursday, everything went wrong.
6. But on Friday, everything went right.
7. Toby played his drums all day Saturday.

Proofreading

Ellen put this note in Roberto's schoolbag. She misspelled three words.
1. Read the note and find each mistake.

> I can't come to your house on Tusday. My piano lesson is on Tuesday this week instead of Wensday. May I come over on Saterday?

2. Write the three misspelled words correctly.

34

Spelling Review

Make believe you are planning a trip. You will be gone for a week. You can go anywhere and do anything you want to. You can go to a different place every day. Write the name of each day. Then tell where you will be and what you will do.

MASTERY WORDS

Follow the directions. Write the Mastery words.
1. Write the words that name the parts of a day.
2. Write the word that means "at this time."
3. Write the word that means "at another time."

Finish the sentences. Use the Mastery words.
4. I go to school in the ___.
5. I come home from school in the ___.
6. A clock never speaks, but it tells ___.

> now
> night
> then
> afternoon
> time
> morning

BONUS WORDS

1. The words <u>day</u> and <u>week</u> are part of some of the Bonus words. Write those words. The <u>y</u> in <u>day</u> is changed to <u>i</u> in one of the words.
2. The word <u>sun</u> is part of two words. Write them.
3. Write the words that tell what comes before and after today.
4. Write the two words that end with <u>ly</u>.
5. Choose four Bonus words that have to do with days. Use those words in a short poem.

> weekend
> weekly
> sunset
> daily
> tomorrow
> sunrise
> daylight
> yesterday

35

9 REVIEW

UNIT 1

apple
bring
else
flag
shall

UNIT 2

add
ill
spell
stuff
unless

Follow these steps as you study each review word.

- Read the word. Name each letter in the word.
- Say the word to yourself. Listen to each sound.
- Copy the word on another piece of paper. Write the word again without looking at your book. Then check what you wrote against the word in your book.
- Practice writing the word until you are <u>sure</u> you know how to spell it.

UNIT 1 Follow the directions. Use the review words.

1. Write the two words that begin with a short vowel sound.
2. Write the three words that have the vowel sound /a/.
3. Write the word that has the vowel sound /i/.

UNIT 2 Write the words that end with these sounds.

4. /l/ (two words) 5. /f/ 6. /d/

Finish the sentences with words from Unit 2.
7. Another word for <u>sick</u> is ____.
8. You ____ <u>un</u> to <u>less</u> to ____ the word ____.

36

UNIT 3   Finish the story with the review words.

Meg was helping her dad __9__ wood. She was carrying logs back to the house. Her puppy ran up. He was barking and __10__ his tail. Meg did not want to __11__ on him. She could not see where she was going. She __12__ and fell on a rock. Meg thought, "I wish that puppy would __13__ when I work."

UNIT 4   Add consonant clusters to these word parts. Write the review words.

14. ___oor   **15.** ___ose
16. ___awer   **17.** ___ing

Write the word from Unit 4 that
18. begins and ends with a cluster.
19. begins with a three-letter cluster.

UNIT 5   Write the words that have these vowel sounds.

20. /a/   **21.** /e/   **22.** /i/ (two words)

Finish the sentences with words from Unit 5.
23. There are lots of sticks lying on the ___.
24. Let's use them to ___ toy boats.
25. Then we'll go to the pond and ___ the boats.

37

UNIT 6 Follow the directions. Use the review words.

26. Write the two words that have the sound /sh/.

27. Write the two words that have the sound /ch/.

28. Write the word that tells how you feel before dinner.

UNIT 7 Follow the directions. Use the review words.

29. Write the three plural words made by adding <u>es</u>. Draw a line under the two letters that come before <u>es</u> in each word.

30. Write the two plural words made by adding <u>s</u>.

Write the word from Unit 7 that goes with each word.

31. aunts   **32.** schools

33. feet   **34.** cameras

UNIT 8 Write the full name for each abbreviation.

35. Sat.   **36.** Wed.

Write the full names of the days that come between these days.

37. Mon.–Wed.   **38.** Wed.–Sat.

39. Thurs.–Sun. **40.** Mon.–Thurs.

38

Writing On Your Own

Read this story beginning. Then look at the picture. It shows how the story ends.

> Funny things are always happening to Robin's cat. One morning the cat was napping on top of Robin's chest of drawers. Robin was getting dressed for school.
>
> The cat was having a dream. You could tell because her paws were moving and her whiskers were twitching. All of a sudden . . .

1. Write a title for the story. Use one of the review words.
2. Finish the story. Tell how Robin's cat got into the drawer. Use as many review words as you can.
3. Pretend that you are Robin and that you are telling your friends what happened to your cat. Write the whole story just the way you would tell it. Tell what you said and did when you saw the cat in the drawer.

39

10 The Sound /j/

1. _giraffe_
2. _danger_
3. _jam_
4. _jug_
5. _juice_
6. _gentle_
7. _giant_
8. _magic_
9. _age_
10. _cage_
11. _large_
12. _page_
13. _bridge_
14. _edge_
15. _judge_

This Week's Words

All the words this week have the sound /j/. Here are four ways to spell /j/.

- with **j** at the beginning of a word
  j̲am

- with **g** before **e** or **i**
  g̲entle   mag̲ic

- with **ge** at the end of a word
  a̲g̲e̲

- with **dge** after short vowel sounds
  e̲d̲g̲e̲

REMEMBER THIS: There is an e̲ at the end of g̲i̲r̲a̲f̲f̲e̲.

Spelling Practice

A. Follow the directions. Use this week's words.

1. Write the three words that start with /j/ spelled g.

2. Write the three words that end with /j/ and have long a.

3. Write the word that ends with /j/ and means the opposite of small.

4. Write the three words that end with /j/ and have short vowel sounds.

B. Add the letter that spells /j/ in each word. Write the words.

5. dan___er

6. ma___ic

C. Tell what the giant is having for breakfast. Write sentences. Use the three words that start with /j/ spelled j and end with another consonant sound. Then circle all the words you used that have the sound /j/.

giraffe
danger
jam
jug
juice
gentle
giant
magic
age
cage
large
page
bridge
edge
judge

41

Spelling and Language

giraffe
danger
jam
jug
juice
gentle
giant
magic
age
cage
large
page
bridge
edge
judge

WRITING SENTENCES

Put the words in order and write four sentences. Remember that a sentence starts with a capital letter and ends with a period.

1. judge   The   went   zoo.   to   gentle   the

2. giant   saw   there.   He   a   giraffe

The keeper said.

3. just   years   giraffe   old."   is   "This   two

The judge said.

4. large   his   for   "He   is   very   age."

Spelling Review

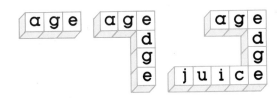

THIS WEEK'S WORDS

Make a "word chain" with this week's words. Write one word.
Use a letter in that word to write another word. Then keep
going, writing words across and down. Try to link up all the
words in one chain. Or you may make more than one chain.

MASTERY WORDS

Follow the directions. Use the Mastery words.
1. Write the word that does not begin with /j/.
2. Write the two words that end with
   consonant clusters.

Write the words with these vowel sounds.
3. /e/   4. /o/   5. /i/

Write the word that goes with each word.
6. ___ rope   7. ___ plane
8. ___ right   9. pickle ___

jar
jet
job
jump
just
give

BONUS WORDS

1. Write the Bonus word that sounds like Jim.
2. Write the words that start with /j/ spelled j.
3. Rewrite the questions. Use Bonus words
   in place of the underlined words.
      What is in the odd box on the shelf?
   Is it spicy cake? Is it chocolate candy?
4. Write the names of other things that might
   be in the box. Use words that have /j/.

join
jungle
gingerbread
gym
package
strange
fudge
ledge

43

11 The Sound /k/

1. kick
2. camp
3. candy
4. cane
5. cost
6. kept
7. key
8. kindness
9. kitten
10. speak
11. back
12. lucky
13. neck
14. pack
15. quick

This Week's Words

All the words this week have the sound /k/. Here are the ways /k/ is spelled.

- with **c** or **k** at the beginning of words
  <u>c</u>amp   <u>k</u>ey

- with **k** after long vowel sounds
  spea<u>k</u>

- with **ck** after short vowel sounds
  ba<u>ck</u>

REMEMBER THIS: The consonant sounds that begin <u>quick</u> are spelled **qu**.

That queer old letter <u>q</u>
Would be quite quiet without a <u>u</u>.
It cannot question or quarrel or quack
Unless a <u>u</u> is right at its back.

44

Spelling Practice

A. Follow the directions. Use this week's words.

1. Write the four words that begin with /k/ spelled <u>c</u>.

2. What vowel letters come after <u>c</u> in these words?

3. Write the five words that begin with /k/ spelled <u>k</u>.

4. What vowel letters come after <u>k</u> in these words?

5. Write the six words that end with /k/. Circle the word that has a long vowel sound.

6. What letter spells /k/ in the word you circled?

B. Finish each sentence. Use this week's words. The underlined name shows how /k/ is spelled in the missing word.

7. <u>Kevin</u> dropped the ____ to his house.

8. <u>Carol</u> saw him drop it near the ____ fire.

9. <u>Vicky</u> was ____ to pick it up and give it back.

10. <u>Chuck</u> said it was ____ Kevin didn't lose it.

kick
camp
candy
cane
cost
kept
key
kindness
kitten
speak
back
lucky
neck
pack
quick

kick
camp
candy
cane
cost
kept
key
kindness
kitten
speak
back
lucky
neck
pack
quick

Spelling and Language

TALKING ABOUT THE PAST

You add <u>ed</u> to most verbs to tell what already happened. Add <u>ed</u> to the underlined words. Finish the answers to the questions.

1. Did you <u>camp</u> in the state park?
   Yes, we ＿＿ there for a week.
2. Did Shelley <u>kick</u> the ball very high?
   Yes, she ＿＿ it over the playground fence.
3. Did Robbie <u>pack</u> his suitcase?
   Yes, he ＿＿ it last night.

Finish the answer to this question. Use one of this week's words.

4. Did Angela <u>keep</u> the dog she found?
   No, she only ＿＿ it until
   the owner came.

The Dictionary

The words in a dictionary are in alphabetical order. If the first letters of words are the same, look at the next letter. <u>Cat</u>, <u>come</u>, <u>cut</u> are in order by the second letter—<u>a</u>, <u>o</u>, <u>u</u>.

Write each group of words in alphabetical order.

1. candy
   kick
   back
   cost
   key

2. lucky
   kindness
   quick
   kept
   speak

46

Spelling Review

camp-stamp

THIS WEEK'S WORDS

Write each of this week's words. Think of a word that rhymes with that word. Then write the rhyming word.

MASTERY WORDS

Follow the directions. Use the Mastery words.
1. Write the three words that begin with the sound /k/.
2. Write the three words that end with /k/.
3. Write the two words that have the sound /i/.

Change the first letter of each word. Write a Mastery word.

4. hold   **5.** hat   **6.** deep
7. peek   **8.** tick   **9.** kick

> **sick**
> **cold**
> **week**
> **keep**
> **cat**
> **pick**

BONUS WORDS

1. Write the six Bonus words that have two or more vowel sounds.
2. Write the two words that begin with consonant clusters.
3. Write the two words that end the way <u>pickle</u> does.
4. Write the two words that end the way <u>ticket</u> does.
5. Write the word that begins and ends with /k/.
6. Write sentences using all the Bonus words. Try to make your sentences tell a story.

> **cabin**
> **camera**
> **creek**
> **jacket**
> **kettle**
> **pocket**
> **smoke**
> **tickle**

47

12 The Sound /s/

1. *six*
2. *city*
3. *police*
4. *suit*
5. *ask*
6. *listen*
7. *decide*
8. *ice*
9. *pencil*
10. *price*
11. *princess*
12. *fence*
13. *once*
14. *piece*
15. *sentence*

This Week's Words

All the words this week have the sound /s/. Here are some ways to spell /s/.

- You can spell /s/ with **s.**
  - <u>s</u>ix   a<u>s</u>k
- You can spell /s/ with **c.**
  - <u>c</u>ity   de<u>c</u>ide
- You can spell /s/ with **ce** at the end of a word.
  - poli<u>ce</u>

One of the words has /s/ spelled another way. Which word is it?

REMEMBER THIS:

There's a <u>t</u> in <u>listen</u>.
That you can see.
But when you say <u>listen</u>,
You don't hear the <u>t</u>.

Spelling Practice

A. Follow the directions. Use this week's words.

1. Write the seven words that end with /s/ spelled <u>ce</u>.

2. Write the word that ends with /s/ spelled <u>ss</u>.

3. Write the two words that tell about the picture. Add <u>s</u> to the end of one of the words.

4. Write the word that ends with a consonant cluster.

5. Write the two words that start with <u>p</u> and have the vowel sound in <u>see</u>.

6. Write the word that has a "silent" letter <u>t</u>.

7. Write the three words that have <u>c</u> before <u>i</u>.

B. Write the verb that goes with these words. Use three different words.

8. ____ a question

9. ____ what to do

10. ____ to the music

six
city
police
suit
ask
listen
decide
ice
pencil
price
princess
fence
once
piece
sentence

49

Spelling and Language

six
city
police
suit
ask
listen
decide
ice
pencil
price
princess
fence
once
piece
sentence

PLURALS

To make most words mean more than one, you add <u>s</u>. You add <u>es</u> to words that end with <u>s</u>, <u>ss</u>, <u>sh</u>, <u>ch</u>, or <u>x</u>.

Finish the sentences with the plurals of this week's words.

1. Mrs. Fong gave Herb a box of colored ____.
2. Mom and Dad both wear ____ to work.
3. Two ____ make twelve.
4. Are the ____ really lower at this store?
5. Rita ate two ____ of fried chicken.
6. All the king's daughters are ____.
7. The farmer put ____ around his fields.
8. All ____ must start with capital letters.

HANDWRITING

d D   g G   q Q

Look at the tails on the **g** and the **q**.

The loop on the **g** turns to the left.

The loop on the **q** turns to the right.

1. Practice writing **d D, g G, q Q** in cursive.

2. Write this sentence: *Did Doug quit?*

Spelling Review

Write some funny story titles. Use this week's words.
Try to use more than one of the words in each title.
Here are some examples: "The Princess and the
Pencil" and "Once Upon a Fence."

MASTERY WORDS

Follow the directions. Use the Mastery words.
1. Write the three words that begin with /s/.
2. Write the three words that end with /s/.
3. Write the three words that have consonant
   clusters.

Finish the sentences. Use the Mastery words.
4. Mr. Witter is a ＿＿ person.
5. He always has a smile on his ＿＿.

face
seed
nice
sent
place
soft

BONUS WORDS

Follow the directions. Use the Bonus words.
1. Write the word that sounds like <u>piece</u>. Then
   use the two words in sentences.
2. Write the word that begins and ends with /s/.
3. Rewrite this sentence: "Are you <u>sure</u> you
   didn't <u>see</u> anything odd?" Use Bonus words in
   place of the underlined words.

Write the Bonus words that go with these words.
4. ＿＿ a poem
5. ride a ＿＿
6. keep a ＿＿
7. ＿＿ spoon

bicycle
certain
notice
peace
recite
secret
silver
since

51

13 Verbs That End with e

1. invite
2. paste
3. skate
4. stare
5. tape
6. taste
7. wipe
8. cared
9. hiked
10. loved
11. moved
12. dancing
13. hoping
14. living
15. smiling

These happy people **smile**.

This Week's Words

The word <u>smile</u> is a verb in this sentence. It ends with the letter <u>e</u>. You can add <u>ed</u> to <u>smile</u> to make a word that tells about the past. When you add <u>ed</u>, you must drop the final <u>e</u>.

These happy people <u>smiled</u>.

You can also add <u>ing</u> to <u>smile</u>. When you add <u>ing</u>, you must also drop the final <u>e</u>.

These happy people are <u>smiling</u>.

All of this week's words are verbs. They all follow this pattern.

smile   smiled   smiling

Spelling Practice

A. Write the verbs that go with the pictures. Use this week's words.

1. _____   2. _____   3. _____

B. Add <u>ed</u> to each of these words.

4. love   **5.** care   **6.** hike   **7.** move

C. Add <u>ing</u> to each of these words.

8. smile   **9.** hope   **10.** dance   **11.** live

D. Finish the sentences. Use this week's words.

12. Did José ____ Beth to his party?
13. It is not polite to ____ at people.
14. Take this sponge and ____ off the table.
15. I watched Mom ____ a bandage on Eva's knee.

E. Try this "word math."

16. dancing − ing = _dance_ + ed = _danced_
17. hiked − ed = ____ + ing = ____
18. hoping − ing = ____ + ed = ____

invite
paste
skate
stare
tape
taste
wipe
cared
hiked
loved
moved
dancing
hoping
living
smiling

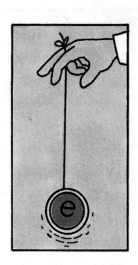

invite
paste
skate
stare
tape
taste
wipe
cared
hiked
loved
moved
dancing
hoping
living
smiling

Spelling and Language

ADDING ed AND ing

You add ed to a word to tell what already happened. You add ing to make a word that can be used with such words as am, is, are, was, and were.

Add ed to the word in dark print. Finish the sentence.

1. **taste**   I have never ____ anything so good.
2. **paste**   Pam ____ silver stars on blue paper.
3. **tape**   Otis carefully ____ the torn page.

Now add ing to the word in dark print.

4. **invite**   Elena is ____ everyone to her house.
5. **skate**   Mark was ____ too fast when he fell.
6. **stare**   What is your cat ____ at?

The Dictionary

Look at this dictionary sample. The entry word is stare. The word with ed and ing comes after stare. To find stared or staring in the dictionary, you must look up stare.

> **stare** /stâr/ v. **stared, staring** To look hard, often without blinking: The dog *stared* at the cat.
> —n. A long, hard look.

Suppose you wanted to find these words in the dictionary. What word would you look up? Write the word.

1. dancing   2. moved   3. hoping
4. cared   5. smiling   6. hiked

54

·S

week are verbs. But some
>uns. See which words can
tence: "This ___ is nice."

This <u>smile</u> is nice.

ds in the blank. If the sentence makes
d is a noun. So write <u>N</u> after the
his paste is nice." So <u>paste</u> can be a
and <u>ing</u> off some of the words.

bicycle

out <u>ed</u>.

ned   **4.** used

ing.

.g   **8.** racing

bake
name
race
save
use
wave

ne must ask questions.

F...is with Mastery words.

9. ...ked a cake.   Leo: What did you ___?
10. Al: I used my head.   Leo: What did you ___?
11. Al: I saved some for you.   Leo: What
did you ___?

BONUS WORDS

1. Add <u>ed</u> and <u>ing</u> to the first four Bonus words.
2. Write the last four words without <u>ed</u> or <u>ing</u>.
3. Write the two words that have long <u>i</u>.
4. Write a story about a birthday party. Try to
   use all the Bonus words in your story.

~~manage~~
~~prepare~~
~~suppose~~
~~surprise~~
divided
promised
behaving
chasing

14 The Vowel Sound /ā/

1. _awake_
2. _brave_
3. _clay_
4. _gate_
5. _hay_
6. _lake_
7. _lay_
8. _mail_
9. _paid_
10. _safe_
11. _snake_
12. _today_
13. _trail_
14. _obey_
15. _eight_

This Week's Words

All the words this week have the vowel sound /ā/. Here are three ways to spell /ā/.

- with **a**-consonant-**e**, as in <u>lake</u>
- with **ai**, as in <u>trail</u>
- with **ay** at the end of a word, as in <u>today</u>

☐ The words <u>obey</u> and <u>eight</u> also have the vowel sound /ā/. How is /ā/ spelled in each of these words?

REMEMBER THIS:

In <u>clay</u> and <u>hay</u> and <u>lay</u> and <u>day</u>,
The letters <u>a</u>-<u>y</u> spell long <u>a</u>.
But <u>obey</u> is spelled another way.
It ends with <u>e</u>-<u>y</u>, just like <u>they</u>.

Then there's <u>gate</u> and <u>late</u>, you see,
Both spelled the same with <u>a</u>-<u>t</u>-<u>e</u>.
So who would expect <u>8</u> to be
Spelled with <u>e</u>-<u>i</u>-<u>g</u>-<u>h</u>-<u>t</u>?

Spelling Practice

A. Follow the directions. Use this week's words.

1. Write the six words that have /ā/ spelled as it is in <u>same</u>.

2. Write the five words that end with /ā/.

3. Circle the word you wrote for **2** that does not end with <u>ay</u>.

4. Write the word that sounds like <u>ate</u>.

B. Write the words that begin and end with these letters.

5. m___l   6. p___d

7. tr___l

C. Finish the story. Use this week's words. The last sound in each word is given to help you. Write one word twice.

Eric and Ed hiked to the __8__ /k/. Next to the __9__ /l/ they saw a __10__ /k/. Ed was afraid, but Eric was __11__ /v/.

"We will be perfectly __12__ /f/. But you must __13__ /ā/ me. Do not make a sound. That __14__ /k/ is not __15__ /k/!"

awake
brave
clay
gate
hay
lake
lay
mail
paid
safe
snake
today
trail
obey
eight

57

Spelling and Language

awake
brave
clay
gate
hay
lake
lay
mail
paid
safe
snake
today
trail
obey
eight

WORD LADDERS

Changing one letter can make a different word. Take clay. Write p in place of c, and you spell play. Start with the words below. Change a letter. The new letter is the first letter in the picture word. The ▲ shows where the new letter goes.

1. <u>t a l e</u>

– – – – ▲

– – ▲ – –

– – – – ▲

2. <u>s a v e</u>

– – – – ▲

– – ▲ – –

– – – – ▲

HANDWRITING

v V x X y Y z Z

The letters **v, x, y,** and **z** begin with this stroke. ___/___

1. Practice writing **v V, x X, y Y, z Z** in cursive.

2. Write this sentence: *Livy saw six zebras.*

58

Spelling Review

Add a-e, ai, or ay to these letters. Write this week's words.

1. tr l
2. aw k
3. cl
4. m l
5. h
6. sn k
7. g t
8. p d
9. l k
10. l
11. br v
12. s f
13. tod

Now write the words that aren't spelled with a-e, ai, or ay.

MASTERY WORDS

Follow the directions. Use the Mastery words.
1. Write the two words that rhyme with day.
2. Circle the word that is not spelled with ay.
3. Use may and they in a sentence.
4. Name two things you need to make a doghouse.

Read each word. Then write two Mastery words that have /ā/ spelled the same way.
5. make
6. train

late
may
nail
paint
same
they

BONUS WORDS

1. Write the three Bonus words that begin with consonant clusters.
2. Write the words that start with de and mis.
3. Write the four words that have /ā/ spelled as it is in train.
4. Name two things that come in purple.
5. Write four sentences. Use two Bonus words in each sentence.

crayon
delay
faint
grape
mistake
railroad
raisin
snail

59

15 The Vowel Sound /ē/

1. _dream_
2. _asleep_
3. _any_
4. _between_
5. _busy_
6. _cheek_
7. _even_
8. _every_
9. _meal_
10. _meat_
11. _only_
12. _really_
13. _seen_
14. _team_
15. _weak_

This Week's Words

All the words this week have the vowel sound /ē/. Here are four ways to spell /ē/.

- with **ea,** as in <u>dream</u>
- with **ee,** as in <u>asleep</u>
- with **e,** as in <u>even</u>
- with **y** at the end of a word, as in <u>any</u>

REMEMBER THIS: You don't always hear the sound of the second <u>e</u> in <u>every</u>. Here's something that can help you remember to put it in.

ever + y = every

Spelling Practice

A. First write the words that go with the pictures. Then follow the directions. Use this week's words.

1. _____

2. _____

3. How is /ē/ spelled in the word you wrote for **1**?

4. Write the other five words that have /ē/ spelled this way.

5. How is /ē/ spelled in the word you wrote for **2**?

6. Write the other three words that have /ē/ spelled this way.

7. Write the word that begins with /ē/.

8. Write the five words that end with /ē/. Circle the word that has /ē/ twice.

B. Finish the sentences. Use this week's words.

9. Jean's six cats keep her very ____.

10. She must feed them each and ____ day.

11. Just ____ you and me, Jean has too many cats.

dream
asleep
any
between
busy
cheek
even
every
meal
meat
only
really
seen
team
weak

61

dream
asleep
any
between
busy
cheek
even
every
meal
meat
only
really
seen
team
weak

Spelling and Language

HOMOPHONES

<u>Sea</u> and <u>see</u> are **homophones.** They sound alike, but they are not spelled alike. They also have different meanings.

Write the homophones for these words.

1. meet   **2.** week

Finish the sentences. Use the homophones.

3. I will ＿＿ you on the corner in an hour.

4. We will buy some ＿＿ for dinner.

5. Akiko did not feel well last ＿＿.

6. She had a cold and felt very ＿＿.

The Dictionary

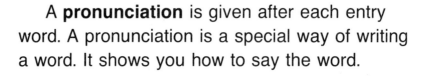

A **pronunciation** is given after each entry word. A pronunciation is a special way of writing a word. It shows you how to say the word.

> **an·y** /en′ē/ *adj.* No special one: *Any* coat will do.

A **pronunciation key** helps you read the pronunciation. It gives all the special signs and the sounds they stand for.

act, āte, câre, ärt;   egg, ēven;   if, īce;   on, ōver, ôr;   bŏŏk, fōōd;   up, tûrn;
ə = a in *ago,* e in *listen,* i in *giraffe,* o in *pilot,* u in *circus;*   yōō = u in *music;*   oil;   out;
chair; sing; shop; thank; that; zh in *treasure.*

Write the word that goes with each pronunciation.

1. /rē′lē/   **2.** /ōn′lē/   **3.** /ev′rē/
4. /mēl/   **5.** /biz′ē/   **6.** /tēm/

Spelling Review

THIS WEEK'S WORDS

Divide the words into groups by the way /ē/ is spelled. You will have four groups: ea, ee, e, and y. Then write as many other words as you can that fit into each group. Remember that really fits into two groups.

MASTERY WORDS

Add ea or ee. Write the Mastery words.

1. fr_ _   2. _ _sy   3. m_ _n
4. d_ _p   5. n_ _t   6. f_ _l

Write Mastery words that mean the opposite.

7. hard   8. kind   9. messy

Write the Mastery words that rhyme with these words.

10. tree   11. keep   12. heel

deep
easy
feel
free
mean
neat

BONUS WORDS

Follow the directions. Use the Bonus words.
1. Write the word that begins with /ē/.
2. Write the two words that end with /ē/.
3. Write the three words that have consonant clusters.
4. Write the two words that are plurals.

Find the Bonus word that rhymes with each word. Then write a sentence using each rhyming pair.

5. beast   6. breeze   7. crazy   8. peace

cozy
daisy
evening
feast
freedom
geese
measles
sneeze

63

16 The Vowel Sound /ī/

1. nine
2. lion
3. bite
4. bright
5. fight
6. hide
7. life
8. line
9. myself
10. prize
11. shy
12. sight
13. tiger
14. wise
15. buy

This Week's Words

All the words this week have the vowel sound /ī/. Here are four ways to spell /ī/.

- with **i**-consonant-**e**, as in <u>nine</u>
- with **igh,** as in <u>bright</u>
- with **i,** as in <u>lion</u>
- with **y** at the end of a word or word part, as in <u>myself</u>

☐ The word <u>buy</u> also has the vowel sound /ī/. What letter are you surprised to find in <u>buy</u>?

REMEMBER THIS: <u>By</u> is a very useful word. It helps you tell where and how. You can sit <u>by</u> the fire. You can win <u>by</u> one point. But to talk about what you'll get at the store, you need <u>buy</u> and <u>buy</u> needs <u>u</u>.

Spelling Practice

A. Follow the directions. Use this week's words.

1. Write the word for the number **9.**
2. Write the six other words that have /ī/ spelled this way.
3. Write the two words that name animals.
4. There are three words you can use to talk about yourself. Write the missing one.
      me, ____, and I
5. Write the two words that rhyme with <u>try</u>. Then circle the word that sounds just like <u>by</u>.
6. Finish the answer to the riddle. Use a word that sounds almost like the first word.
   What do you call a big cat that tells fibs?
      A lying ____.

B. Write the words that end with /t/ and begin with these letters.

7. f   **8.** br   **9.** s

C. Write the words that go with these words. Use this week's words.

10. ____ and seek   **11.** pillow ____
12. all by ____   **13.** ____ and sell

nine
lion
bite
bright
fight
hide
life
line
myself
prize
shy
sight
tiger
wise
buy

Spelling and Language

nine
lion
bite
bright
fight
hide
life
line
myself
prize
shy
sight
tiger
wise
buy

RHYMING WORDS

Finish the poem with words that rhyme with the words in dark print. Use this week's words.

It was a calm and starry **night.**
The moon was very __1__ .
On this night so warm and **fine,**
As the clock was striking __2__ ,
I met a frog, quite by **surprise,**
Who looked very old and __3__ .
As he chewed upon a **fly,**
He asked me why I was so __4__ .
Then he grinned a grin so **wide**
That I had to run and __5__ .
And I laughed with all my **might**
At this strange and silly __6__ .

HANDWRITING

n N m M

The letter **n** touches the midline two times. n

The letter **m** touches the midline three times. m

1. Practice writing **n N, m M** in cursive.

2. Write this sentence: *I went to Maine.*

Spelling Review

THIS WEEK'S WORDS

Write sentences using all of this week's words. Try to use more than one of the words in each sentence. Here is an example: "The <u>shy</u> <u>tiger</u> tried to <u>hide</u>."

MASTERY WORDS

Write the Mastery words that mean the opposite of these words.

1. left   **2.** narrow   **3.** lose   **4.** low

Finish each sentence. Use a Mastery word. Then find the other word in the sentence that has /ī/ spelled the same way. Write that word.

5. Maria rides her ___ to school.
6. Tell me ___ you need my help.
7. Is it all ___ if I turn on the light?
8. The sun is bright and ___ in the sky.
9. Kind people helped us ___ our lost dog.
10. The rug is nine feet long and six feet ___.

bike
find
high
right
why
wide

BONUS WORDS

1. Write the Bonus words that have /ī/ spelled with <u>i-e</u>. Use each word in a sentence.
2. Write the words that have /ī/ spelled with <u>i</u>. Use each word in a sentence.
3. Add a word with /ī/ to each of these word parts. Write four Bonus words.

a	way	de	mid

awhile
delight
highway
midnight
pirate
polite
quite
title

17 The Vowel Sound /ō/

1. both
2. float
3. blow
4. fold
5. follow
6. hello
7. joke
8. load
9. old
10. rose
11. sold
12. spoke
13. stove
14. window
15. bow

/bōth flōt/

This Week's Words

All the words this week have the vowel sound /ō/. Here are four ways to spell /ō/.

- with **o**-consonant-**e,** as in joke
- with **oa,** as in <u>float</u>
- with **o,** as in <u>both</u>
- with **ow** at the end of a word, as in <u>blow</u>

REMEMBER THIS: The word <u>bow</u> can be said two ways. <u>Bow</u> has /ō/ when you say "Tie the ribbon in a <u>bow</u>." <u>Bow</u> has the vowel sound heard in <u>cow</u> when you say "Take a <u>bow</u>." But either way, it is spelled the same: <u>bow</u>.

Spelling Practice

A. Follow the directions. Use this week's words.

1. Write the four words that have /ō/ spelled as it is in <u>nose</u>.
2. Write the five words that end with /ō/.
3. Circle the word you wrote for **2** that does not end with <u>ow</u>.
4. Write the three words that end with the cluster <u>ld</u>.
5. Write the word that means "two."

B. Write the words that go with these pronunciations.

6. /flōt/   7. /lōd/

C. Finish the sentences. Use this week's words. The other words in the sentence will help you decide which word to use. Use one word twice.

8. Pablo called me on the phone to say ____.
9. He told me a funny ____ about an elephant.
10. He said, "What's big and gray and has a trunk and a rear ____?"
11. I said, "An ____ gray car."
12. He said, "No, an elephant. I made up the part about the ____."
13. We ____ laughed a lot.

both
float
blow
fold
follow
hello
joke
load
old
rose
sold
spoke
stove
window
bow

both
float
blow
fold
follow
hello
joke
load
old
rose
sold
spoke
stove
window
bow

Spelling and Language

USING VERBS

Finish the answers to these questions. Use this week's words. You will write verbs that tell what already happened.

1. How much lemonade did Lucy sell?
   She ____ twenty glasses of lemonade.
2. When did the sun rise today?
   The sun ____ at 5:35.
3. Did you speak with Grandma yesterday?
   Yes, I ____ with her on the telephone.

Write a question for this answer. Use one of this week's words.

4. Jeff blew up ten balloons.

Proofreading

Doug wrote this secret message. It tells Kim where he hid the peanuts. Doug misspelled six words.

1. Read the message and find Doug's mistakes.

Stand under the front windo. Take six steps toward the roze garden. Point boath feet east. Follo your nose to the old tree. Look for a yellow boe. This is no joak.

2. Write the six misspelled words correctly.

Spelling Review

heavy load

load the car

1. Write NOUN and VERB at the top of your paper.
2. Write each of this week's words under the right word. A word such as <u>load</u> can be a noun or a verb. But write it in just one place. (<u>Both</u>, <u>hello</u>, and <u>old</u> are not nouns or verbs.)
3. Think of a describing word that goes with each noun. Write the two words. Here's an example: <u>funny joke</u>.
4. Then think of a noun that goes with each verb. Write the words. Here are examples: <u>corks float</u> and <u>fold the paper</u>.

MASTERY WORDS

1. Write the three Mastery words that end with /ō/.
2. Circle the word you wrote that means "too."
3. Write the two words that begin with /ō/.
4. Write the word that rhymes with <u>nose</u>.
5. Use the word you just wrote in a sentence.

> **also**
> **grow**
> **low**
> **oak**
> **own**
> **those**

BONUS WORDS

Follow the directions. Use the Bonus words.
1. Write all the words in alphabetical order.
2. After each word write the spelling for /ō/.

Try this "word math."
3. <u>three</u> − /ē/ + /ō/ + <u>t</u> = _____
4. <u>say</u> − /ā/ + <u>tea</u> − /ē/ + <u>roll</u> = _____
5. <u>show</u> − /ō/ + <u>ad</u> + /ō/ = _____

Now make up your own "word math" problems.
Use the Bonus words.

> **slope**
> **vote**
> **boast**
> **throat**
> **narrow**
> **shadow**
> **scold**
> **stroll**

18 REVIEW

UNIT 10

juice
giant
danger
large
bridge

UNIT 11

kept
key
speak
quick
lucky

Follow these steps as you study each review word.

- Read the word. Name each letter in the word.
- Say the word to yourself. Listen to each sound.
- Copy the word on another piece of paper. Write the word again without looking at your book. Then check what you wrote against the word in your book.
- Practice writing the word until you are <u>sure</u> you know how to spell it.

UNIT 10 Follow the directions. Use the review words.

1. Write the two words that begin with /j/.
2. Write the two words that end with /j/.
3. Write the word for a reason to be afraid.

UNIT 11 Follow the directions. Use the review words.

4. Write the three words that have the vowel sound /ē/.
5. Write the two words that have consonant clusters.
6. Write the word for someone who has good fortune.
7. Write the word that is the opposite of <u>slow</u>.

UNIT 12 Follow the directions. Use the review words.

8. Write the word that has a "silent" letter t̲.
9. Write the word that begins and ends with /s/.

Write the words that have almost the same meaning as these words. Use words from Unit 12.

10. pen
11. hear
12. town
13. slice

UNIT 13 Add e̲d̲ or i̲n̲g̲ to these words. Write the words.

14. care + ed
15. invite + ed
16. taste + ing
17. smile + ing

Finish the sentences. Use words from Unit 13.

18. Barb and Rick can ___ very well.
19. Mom said I may ___ you to stay for dinner.
20. Did you ever ___ my aunt's carrot cake?

UNIT 14 Write the words that have /ā/ spelled as it is in these words.

May Dave sail?
21 22 23

Write the words that go with the pronunciations.

24. /āt/
25. /ō·bā′/
26. /brāv/
27. /māl/

UNIT 12
listen
city
pencil
piece
sentence

UNIT 13
invite
skate
taste
cared
smiling

UNIT 14
brave
mail
today
eight
obey

73

UNIT 15 Follow the directions. Use the review words.

28. Write the two words that end with /ē/.
29. Write the word that sounds like <u>week</u>.

Add letters for /ē/ to these letters. Write the words.

30. t___m   31. betw___n

UNIT 16 Change the underlined letter or letters in each word. Write the review words.

32. li<u>ne</u>   33. <u>f</u>right
34. <u>w</u>ide   35. <u>it</u>self

Use <u>by</u> or <u>buy</u> to finish each sentence.

36. I went to the store all ___ myself.
37. I went to ___ a present for Dad.

UNIT 17 Write words that are the opposites of these words.

38. lead   39. good-by   40. sink

Finish the sentences. Use review words from Unit 17.

  __41__ these directions. Hold this stick with __42__ hands. Stamp your foot and cough. What's the matter? Can't you get your motorcycle started?
  Isn't that a funny __43__ ?

74

Writing On Your Own

Look at these pictures.

1. Put the pictures in order. The one marked **A** is the first one. Number the others 2, 3, 4.
2. Write a sentence about each picture. Use as many review words as you can.
3. Pretend that you are the lion. Write a story about the pictures. Tell the story the way the lion might tell it. Use as many review words as you can.

19 Compound Words

1. anyone
2. anyway
3. bedroom
4. cannot
5. everybody
6. football
7. grandfather
8. grandmother
9. herself
10. himself
11. maybe
12. outside
13. playground
14. sometimes
15. yourself

This Week's Words

Sometimes two words are put together to make a new word. The new word is called a **compound word.**

All the words this week are compound words. Remember how the smaller words that make up each word are spelled. That will make writing the long word easier.

76

Spelling Practice

A. Follow the directions. Use this week's words.

1. Add a word from the red box to a word in the green box. Write six compound words.

bed	may
play	can
foot	some

ball	not
room	be
times	ground

2. Write two different words made from <u>any</u> and another word.

3. Write three words made from <u>self</u> and another word.

4. Write the two words that name your parent's parents.

5. The first word rhymes with <u>day</u>. The second word rhymes with <u>sound</u>. Write the compound word. Then write the three consonant clusters in the word.

B. Change one of the words in each compound. Make a word that means the opposite.

6. inside   **7.** nobody

C. Finish the sentences. Use this week's words.

Hector fell and hurt __8__. Kathy fell and hurt __9__. Did you fall and hurt __10__, too?

anyone
anyway
bedroom
cannot
everybody
football
grandfather
grandmother
herself
himself
maybe
outside
playground
sometimes
yourself

Spelling and Language

ONE WORD OR TWO

In the sentence "Maybe I'll see you tomorrow," you write maybe as one word. But in the sentence "I may be here tomorrow," you write may be as two words. The same thing happens with anyway and any way. It is one word in the sentence "I didn't want it anyway." But it is two words in "You may color the picture any way you like."

Finish the sentences with maybe or may be.
1. ___ this path leads to the zoo.
2. This ___ a shorter way to the zoo.

Finish the sentences with anyway or any way.
3. Is there ___ we can help you?
4. We will try to help you ___.

The Dictionary

The words in a dictionary are listed in alphabetical order. Use this week's words. Write the word that would come right after each of these words in the spelling dictionary.
1. grand   2. plant   3. become   4. follow
5. cane   6. here   7. hike   8. ourselves

Look up each word in the spelling dictionary and check your answers.

78

Spelling Review

THIS WEEK'S WORDS

Add the missing words. Write the compound words that are this week's words.

1. can + ____
2. your + ____
3. ____ + way
4. ____ + side
5. foot + ____
6. ____ + room
7. her + ____
8. ____ + times
9. play + ____
10. him + ____
11. ____ + be
12. ____ + one
13. ____ + father
14. every + ____
15. ____ + mother

MASTERY WORDS

1. Write two Mastery words made from <u>in</u> and another word.
2. Write two Mastery words made from <u>one</u> and another word.
3. Match the words. Write three Mastery words.

   with   any   in   thing   side   out

into
anything
everyone
someone
without
inside

BONUS WORDS

1. Write the Bonus word that does not sound like the two words it is made from.
2. Write four words made with <u>ever</u> or <u>every</u>.
3. Replace the underlined words with Bonus words. Then finish the story.

   Jason looked <u>in all places</u> for the lost whistle. <u>At the same time</u> I searched <u>on the floor below</u>. We told <u>our own minds</u> that it was lost <u>for the rest of time</u>. But then . . .

everyday
forever
meanwhile
downstairs
everywhere
cupboard
whoever
ourselves

20 Contractions

1. can't
2. didn't
3. don't
4. he's
5. I'll
6. I'm
7. isn't
8. it's
9. let's
10. she's
11. that's
12. there's
13. we'll
14. we're
15. won't

This Week's Words

A **contraction** is a short way of writing two words together. Some of the letters are left out. An **apostrophe** takes their place.

Can't is the contraction of can and not. The apostrophe takes the place of n and o.

All the words this week are contractions. What words make up the contractions? What letters are left out?

REMEMBER THIS:

How do not becomes don't is easy to tell.
But will not to won't—what happens then?
Why, the i runs away with the double l,
And the o jumps over the n.

80

Spelling Practice

A. Write the contractions of these words.

1. I will

2. we will

3. let us

4. we are

5. I am

B. Follow the directions. Use this week's words.

6. Write the five words that are contractions of <u>not</u> and another word.

7. Write the six words that are contractions of <u>is</u> and another word.

8. Rewrite this sentence twice. Use <u>it's</u> the first time. Use <u>isn't</u> the second time.

It is not raining now.

C. Rewrite each sentence. Use two contractions in each one.

9. We are sure he did not see us.

10. Linda will not tell us what she is making.

11. We will be late if we do not hurry.

81

can't
didn't
don't
he's
I'll
I'm
isn't
it's
let's
she's
that's
there's
we'll
we're
won't

Spelling and Language

WRITING NEGATIVE SENTENCES

I can't sing means the opposite of I can sing. They didn't sing means the opposite of They sang. I can't sing and They didn't sing are negative sentences.

Use one of this week's words. Make each sentence into a negative sentence.
1. The weather is very nice today.
2. Maria and Gilda will play in the park.
3. They want to play in the rain.

Proofreading

1. Read the letter Darin wrote to his grandmother. Find the six spelling mistakes he made.

> Dear Grandma,
>   We'r coming to visit you next month. Thats what Mom said today. I donn't know when we'll get there. Dad says hes going to call you.
>   I'm going to bed now. I'l write again soon.
>   Love,
>   Darin

2. Write the six misspelled words correctly.

82

Spelling Review

THIS WEEK'S WORDS

Use all of this week's words in sentences. Draw a line under the contraction in each sentence. After the sentence, write the two words that make up the contraction. Here is an example.

    I <u>can't</u> find my mittens.   can not

MASTERY WORDS

Write the two words that make up each contraction.
1. isn't   **2.** don't   **3.** there's   **4.** won't

<u>There</u> tells where. <u>Their</u> tells whose. Finish the sentences. Use <u>there</u> or <u>their</u>.
5. Peg and Brian invited me to ____ house.
6. I was ____ all afternoon.
7. I had fun playing with ____ dog.

do
is
not
their
there
will

BONUS WORDS

Follow the directions. Use the Bonus words.
1. Use <u>their</u>, <u>there</u>, and <u>they're</u> in sentences.
2. Use <u>your</u> and <u>you're</u> in sentences.
3. Write the word that is a contraction of <u>is</u> and another word.

Answer these questions. Use a contraction made from <u>not</u> and another word in each answer.
4. Have you eaten?   **5.** Were you there?
6. Does Paul like nuts?   **7.** Were they sad?
8. Are we next?

aren't
doesn't
haven't
they're
wasn't
weren't
what's
you're

21 The Sounds /ô/ and /ôr/

1. straw
2. horse
3. born
4. cause
5. corn
6. course
7. four
8. horn
9. jaw
10. north
11. short
12. talk
13. taught
14. walk
15. wash

This Week's Words

The sound /ô/ is heard in <u>straw</u>. It can be spelled with these letters.

- **a,** as in <u>talk</u>
- **aw,** as in <u>straw</u>
- **au,** as in <u>cause</u>

The sounds /ôr/ are heard in <u>horse</u>. The sound /ô/ with <u>r</u> can be spelled with these letters.

- **or,** as in <u>horse</u>
- **our,** as in <u>course</u>

Spelling Practice

A. Follow the directions. Use this week's words.

1. Write the two words that have /ô/ spelled as it is in <u>paw</u>.

2. Write the word that sounds like <u>for</u>.

3. Write the six words that have /ôr/ spelled as it is in <u>for</u>.

4. Write the other word that has /ôr/ spelled as it is in <u>four</u>.

5. Write the word that rhymes with <u>caught</u>.

6. Write the three words that have the vowel sound spelled with <u>a</u>. Circle the words that have a "silent" letter <u>l</u>.

straw
horse
born
cause
corn
course
four
horn
jaw
north
short
talk
taught
walk
wash

B. Add the letters that spell /ô/ and /ôr/. Write the words that finish the story.

A unicorn looks like a **(7)** h＿se. But it has a long, straight **(8)** h＿n on its forehead. Unicorns like to **(9)** w＿sh their horns in water. This makes the water magic for a **(10)** sh＿t time. It can **(11)** c＿se people to have good luck. Of **(12)** c＿se, there is really no such thing as a unicorn.

85

straw
horse
born
cause
corn
course
four
horn
jaw
north
short
talk
taught
walk
wash

Spelling and Language

NOUNS AND VERBS

A **noun** names a person, a place, or a thing. A **verb** shows action or being. Finish each pair of sentences with one of this week's words. The word will be a verb in the first sentence and a noun in the second.

1. Rob and Dad ____ the clothes every Saturday.
2. When the ____ is done, they have lunch.
3. Aunt Ann always listens when I ____ to her.
4. I feel good after a long ____ with her.
5. Jaime and Camille ____ to school.
6. They always enjoy their ____ to school.

The Dictionary

A **definition** tells what a word means. Some words have more than one definition. Read the definitions for the word <u>cause</u>. One is a noun (<u>n.</u>). The other is a verb (<u>v.</u>).

> **cause** /kôz/ *n.* A person or thing that makes something happen; reason: He was the *cause* of the trouble.
> — *v.* **caused, causing** To make something happen: A traffic jam *caused* us to be late.

Write <u>n.</u> or <u>v.</u> to show how <u>cause</u> is used each time.
1. What could have <u>caused</u> Taro to stay at home?
2. No one knows the <u>cause</u> of the fire.
3. You have no <u>cause</u> to be angry.
4. Heavy rains can <u>cause</u> flooding.

Spelling Review

THIS WEEK'S WORDS

Make a "word chain" with this week's words. Write one word. Use a letter in that word to write another word. Then keep going, writing words across and down. Try to link up all the words in one chain. Or you may make more than one chain.

MASTERY WORDS

Follow the directions. Use the Mastery words.
1. Write the two words that have /ô/ spelled a.
2. Write the two words that have /ô/ spelled aw.
3. Write the two words that have the sounds /ôr/.

Write the words that are the opposite of these words.
4. less   5. after   6. short

before
crawl
draw
fall
more
tall

BONUS WORDS

Write a Bonus word to go with each definition.
1. girl child   2. place for horses
3. rainstorm   4. baby deer
5. place for a judge   6. seed of oak trees

Follow the directions. Use the Bonus words.
7. Write the word that sounds like paws.
8. Write the word with a "silent" letter l.
9. Use the Bonus words in sentences. Try to make your sentences tell a story.

acorn
corral
court
daughter
downpour
fawn
pause
stalk

22 The Sounds /ûr/

1. sir
2. fur
3. learn
4. world
5. birthday
6. bluebird
7. burn
8. circle
9. early
10. earn
11. earth
12. heard
13. return
14. skirt
15. worry

The early bird catches the purple worm.

This Week's Words

The sound /û/ with <u>r</u> is heard in all the words this week. Here are four ways to spell /ûr/.

- with **ir,** as in <u>bird</u> and <u>sir</u>
- with **ur,** as in <u>purple</u> and <u>fur</u>
- with **ear,** as in <u>early</u> and <u>learn</u>
- with **or,** as in <u>worm</u> and <u>world</u>

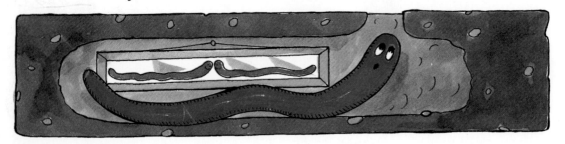

Spelling Practice

A. Follow the directions. Use this week's words.

1. Write the words that have /ûr/ spelled the same as it is in these words.

2. Write the compound word made from <u>bird</u> and another word.

3. Write the four other words that have /ûr/ spelled <u>ir</u>.

4. Circle the compound word you wrote for **3.**

5. Write the three words that begin with /ûr/.

6. Put a letter in front of <u>earn</u>. Write another word.

7. Answer this question. Use one of this week's words.

   Did you hear the phone ring?
   Yes, ____

B. Write the words that have these meanings. Use this week's words.

8. find out

9. come back

10. too soon

11. round shape

sir
fur
learn
world
birthday
bluebird
burn
circle
early
earn
earth
heard
return
skirt
worry

89

Spelling and Language

sir
fur
learn
world
birthday
bluebird
burn
circle
early
earn
earth
heard
return
skirt
worry

RHYMING WORDS

Finish the poem with words that rhyme with the words in dark print. Use this week's words. You will write one word twice. Remember, /ûr/ can be spelled in different ways.

Late one night, something **stirred.**
What could have made the noise I __1__?
I crept downstairs, I did not **hurry.**
I was filled with fear and __2__.
Something was hiding behind a **fern.**
What could it be? I had to __3__.
Then I heard something **purr,**
And I touched something's __4__.
It was just my cat, small and **furry,**
That caused me so much fear and __5__.

Proofreading

Keisha wrote this report about raccoons. She misspelled five words.

1. Read the report and find each mistake.

Raccoons have thick fir. They have black curcles around their tails. They hunt at night and retearn to their dens erly in the morning. Baby raccoons stay with their mother. They lurn from her how to hunt and climb trees.

2. Write the five misspelled words correctly.

Spelling Review

THIS WEEK'S WORDS

In place of /ûr/, write the letters that spell /ûr/. Write each word.

1. sûr
2. retûrn
3. skûrt
4. bûrn
5. bûrthday
6. fûr
7. cûrcle
8. ûrth
9. lûrn
10. bluebûrd
11. ûrn
12. wûrry
13. ûrly
14. hûrd
15. wûrld

MASTERY WORDS

bird
hurt
work
turn
girl
word

1. Write the Mastery word that begins with t. Write the word that ends with t. Then write two other letters that are alike in the words.
2. Write the two words that have the letters or.
3. What could you call doing your spelling? Write two words.
4. My friend Holly has a parrot named Polly. Write the words that tell what Holly is and what Polly is.

BONUS WORDS

pearl
purpose
search
thirsty
turtle
whirl
worst
worth

1. Write the Bonus word that goes with hungry.
2. What animal carries its house on its back? Write the name.
3. Write the word that means "seek, or look for."
4. Write the word that is the opposite of best.
5. Next to each word you wrote for 1–4, write another word that has /ûr/ spelled the same.
6. Use all the Bonus words in sentences. Try to make your sentences tell a story.

91

23 The Sounds /är/ and /âr/

1. park
2. stairs
3. art
4. bark
5. barn
6. card
7. farm
8. yard
9. air
10. fair
11. hair
12. pair
13. bear
14. pear
15. heart

This Week's Words

The sound /är/ is heard in <u>park</u>. It is usually spelled **ar.** ☐ But in <u>heart</u>, /är/ is spelled **ear.**

The sound /âr/ is heard in <u>stairs</u>. It is often spelled **air.** But /âr/ can also be spelled **ear,** as in <u>bear</u>.

REMEMBER THIS: Here's a way to remember the <u>e</u> in <u>heart</u>. "You can <u>hear</u> your <u>heart</u>." The first four letters in <u>heart</u> are the letters that spell <u>hear</u>.

Spelling Practice

A. Follow the directions. Use this week's words.

1. Write the word for something you cannot see but is all around you.

2. Add one letter at a time to the word you wrote for **1**. Write three words.

3. Write the two words that sound alike.

4. Write the word that sounds like <u>stares</u>.

5. Write two words that rhyme with <u>wear</u> and are spelled with <u>ear</u>.

6. Answer this riddle. Use two words that rhyme. What do you call a panda's fur?

B. Write two words that rhyme with each of these words.

7. dark

8. hard

9. part

C. Add one letter to the end of each word. Write some of this week's words.

10. car

11. far

12. bar (two words)

park
stairs
art
bark
barn
card
farm
yard
air
fair
hair
pair
bear
pear
heart

93

park
stairs
art
bark
barn
card
farm
yard
air
fair
hair
pair
bear
pear
heart

Spelling and Language

MAKING COMPOUND WORDS

Two words can be put together to make a new word. The new word is called a **compound word.**

back	board	house	plane	up

Put some of this week's words together with words from the box. Make compound words to go with these definitions.

1. It flies in the sky.
2. It is behind the house.
3. You climb the steps to get there.
4. It is where the farmer lives.
5. It is what boxes are made from.

The Dictionary

The words in a dictionary are in alphabetical order. If the first letters of words are the same, look at the second letter. If the second letters are the same, look at the third letter. Back, bad, bag are in order by third letter — c, d, g.

Write each group of words in alphabetical order.

1. pear
   stairs
   park
   straw
   pair

2. heart
   farm
   herself
   hair
   fair

road
robin
rock
rode

94

Spelling Review

THIS WEEK'S WORDS

Use all the words to make a word search puzzle. You can write the words across or down. Fill in the empty spaces with other letters. Then let someone else solve it.

MASTERY WORDS

Change one letter in each word. Write Mastery words.

1. bark   **2.** card   **3.** car   **4.** art

Add letters to these words. Write Mastery words.

5. art   **6.** air

Follow the directions. Write the words.

7. Take away the first letter in <u>farm</u>.

8. Take away the last letter in <u>farm</u>.

Write the Mastery words that mean the opposite.

9. soft   **10.** light

BONUS WORDS

Write the Bonus words that go with these words.

1. ___ clock **2.** ___ shop **3.** flea ___ **4.** rose ___

Follow the directions. Use the Bonus words.

5. Write the two words that have the sounds /âr/.

6. Write all the words in alphabetical order.

7. Write a story about an artist and a barber. Use all the Bonus words in your story.

24 More Plurals

1. pancakes
2. ears
3. eyes
4. grades
5. lands
6. marbles
7. newspapers
8. shapes
9. wheels
10. buddies
11. butterflies
12. fairies
13. guppies
14. puppies
15. spies

This Week's Words

A **plural noun** names more than one thing. You add <u>s</u> to most nouns to make the plural.

pancake	pancakes
ear	ears

Just <u>s</u> is not enough for words like <u>buddy</u> and <u>spy</u>. These words end with a consonant and <u>y</u>. To make them plural, change <u>y</u> to <u>i</u> and add <u>es</u>.

buddy	buddies
spy	spies

Spelling Practice

A. Write the plural of each word.

1. guppy   **2.** fairy   **3.** buddy   **4.** spy

B. Write the plural of the words in dark print.
Finish the sentences.

5. newspaper   Mr. Ito reads ten ____ every
           day.
6. land   Some are sent to him from other ____.

C. Write the singular of these words.

7. grades   **8.** pancakes
9. shapes   **10.** marbles

D. Write the singular and plural words for
each picture.

pancakes
ears
eyes
grades
lands
marbles
newspapers
shapes
wheels
buddies
butterflies
fairies
guppies
puppies
spies

11.   **12.**   **13.**

E. Write the plural of the words in dark print.
Finish the sentences.

14. eye   He has ____ in the back of his head.
15. ear   Tell me — I'm all ____.

pancakes
ears
eyes
grades
lands
marbles
newspapers
shapes
wheels
buddies
butterflies
fairies
guppies
puppies
spies

Spelling and Language

SINGULAR AND PLURAL NOUNS

One of this week's words will finish each sentence. Decide if the singular or plural word fits. For example, <u>puppies</u> fits the sentence "Those ___ wag their tails." But <u>puppy</u> fits the sentence "That ___ wags its tail." Write the words that fit the sentences.

1. A caterpillar becomes a beautiful ___.
2. Jay's ___ get better with each report card.
3. My dog's ___ are long and floppy.
4. A circle and a square are two different ___.

Proofreading

Jill wrote this in her diary. She misspelled six words and forgot two capital letters.

1. Find each of Jill's mistakes.

We had panacakes for breakfast. After breakfast I fed my gubbies and counted my marbels. My buddie Todd came over. We decided to paint my old wagon. we put newpapers down on the back porch. now the wagon is purple and the wheals are yellow.

2. Write the six misspelled words correctly.
3. Copy what Jill wrote in your best handwriting. Spell the words correctly. Use capital letters correctly.

98

Spelling Review

THIS WEEK'S WORDS

Write some funny story titles. Use this week's words.
Try to use more than one of the words in each title.
You may use the singular or the plural. Here are
some examples: "Why Wheels Are That Shape"
and "Life with Puppies and Guppies."

MASTERY WORDS

Follow the directions. Use the Mastery words.
1. Write the three words that name things in
   the picture.
2. Write the word that has the sound /ē/.

Finish the sentences. Use the Mastery words.
3. Jenny played with her electric ____.
4. Then she watered the ____ in her room.
5. Next, she pumped up the ____ on her bike.

trains
tires
streets
stones
plants
ants

BONUS WORDS

1. Write the singular of each Bonus word.
   Tell what happens to make the word plural.
2. Write the two compound words.
3. Write the five words that have double letters.
4. Write the six words with long vowel sounds.
5. Write sentences using the Bonus words. Try
   to use two of the words in each sentence.

blueberries
stories
cartwheels
chances
cherries
details
hobbies
puddles

25 "Silent" Letters

1. _knee_
2. _knew_
3. _knit_
4. _knock_
5. _knot_
6. _known_
7. _calf_
8. _half_
9. _climb_
10. _lamb_
11. _thumb_
12. _wren_
13. _written_
14. _wrote_
15. _ghost_

/Knē/

This Week's Words

Say the word <u>knee</u>. Listen to the beginning sound /n/. Hundreds of years ago, people said both /k/ and /n/ at the beginning of <u>knee</u>. Now the sound /k/ is not heard. But the letter <u>k</u> is still written. When the sound of a letter is not heard, we call it a "silent" letter.

Read each of the words to yourself. Decide which letter is a "silent" letter in each word.

Spelling Practice

A. Follow the directions. Use this week's words.

1. Write the three words that begin with the sound /r/.
2. Write the three words that end with the sound /m/.
3. Write the two words that have a "silent" letter l.
4. Write the word that has a "silent" h.

B. Write this week's words to go with these pronunciations.

5. /nit/   6. /nok/   7. /nē/   8. /not/

C. Write this week's words that rhyme with these words.

9. jam   10. time   11. hum

D. Read the first sentence in each group. Find the word that has a "silent" letter. Then finish the next two sentences. Use words that have the same "silent" letter.

12. Luis and Cissy know how to solve the puzzle.
    I should have ___ they'd figure it out.
    I wish I ___ how they did it so quickly.
13. Debbie writes long letters to Mary Jane.
    The one she ___ today was longer than usual.
    It may be the longest letter she's ever ___.

knee
knew
knit
knock
knot
known
calf
half
climb
lamb
thumb
wren
written
wrote
ghost

101

knee
knew
knit
knock
knot
known
calf
half
climb
lamb
thumb
wren
written
wrote
ghost

Spelling and Language

NOUNS AND VERBS

A **noun** names a person, a place, or a thing. A **verb** shows action or being. Finish each pair of sentences with one of this week's words. The word will be a verb in the first sentence and a noun in the second.

1. Just ____ on the door when you get here.
2. I will come out as soon as I hear your ____.
3. Let's ____ up the mountain on Saturday.
4. It's a rough ____, so wear heavy shoes.
5. It was a mistake to ____ the string.
6. Now I can't get the ____ out.

The Dictionary

Two **guide words** appear at the top of every dictionary page. The word on the left is the first word on the page. The word on the right is the last word. All the other words on the page are in alphabetical order between the guide words.

trail	until
trail /trāl/ *n.* **1** A path. **2** The marks left by a person or animal. —*v.* To follow behind: Jacob *trailed*	**Tues.** Abbreviation for *Tuesday.* **Tues·day** /t(y)o͞oz′dē *or* t(y)o͞oz′dā/ *n.* The third day of the week.

Pretend that these are pairs of guide words. Write two of this week's words that would be on each page.

1. **cabin   color**
2. **game   help**
3. **kind   knife**
4. **lake   truck**

102

Spelling Review

THIS WEEK'S WORDS

What two letters are needed to finish the words? Add the letters and write this week's words.

1. _ _ost
2. thu_ _
3. _ _ock
4. _ _it
5. la_ _
6. _ _en
7. ca_ _
8. _ _ot
9. _ote
10. _ _ee
11. cli_ _
12. _ _own
13. _ _ew
14. ha_ _
15. _ _itten

MASTERY WORDS

know
listen
should
walk
who
write

Follow the directions. Use the Mastery words.
1. Write the three words that start with the letter w.
2. Write the word that starts with the sound /r/.
3. Write a question. Start with the word that rhymes with you.

Add the "silent" letters. Write Mastery words.
4. lis_en
5. _now
6. shou_d
7. wa_k

BONUS WORDS

crumbs
chalk
knead
kneel
knife
limb
wreck
wrist

Write the Bonus words for each pronunciation.
1. /nēl/
2. /rek/
3. /lim/
4. /nēd/
5. /krumz/
6. /rist/
7. /chôk/
8. /nīf/

Follow the directions. Use the Bonus words.
9. Write the word that sounds like need. Use both words in a sentence.
10. Write a story about Silent Kay, the girl who never talked. Use as many words as you can that start with kn.

26 Number Words

1. *first*
2. *second*
3. *third*
4. *fourth*
5. *fifth*
6. *sixth*
7. *seventh*
8. *eighth*
9. *ninth*
10. *tenth*
11. *twenty*
12. *thirty*
13. *forty*
14. *fifty*
15. *hundred*

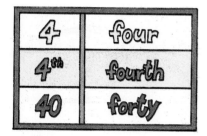

This Week's Words

Number words like <u>first</u>, <u>second</u>, and <u>third</u> tell the order of things. Many of these words are made by adding <u>th</u> to a number word.

four + th = fourth

A letter is dropped before <u>th</u> is added to <u>eight</u> and <u>nine</u>.

eigh|t| + th = eigh|_|th = eighth
nin|e| + th = nin|_|th = ninth

Look at the word <u>fifth</u>. What happens to <u>five</u> to make <u>fifth</u>?

REMEMBER THIS: There is a <u>u</u> in <u>four</u> and <u>fourth</u> but not in <u>forty</u>.

Spelling Practice

first
second
third
fourth
fifth
sixth
seventh
eighth
ninth
tenth
twenty
thirty
forty
fifty
hundred

A. Write the missing number words in each group.

1. sixth, ____, eighth, ____
2. ten, ____, thirty, ____
3. fourth, sixth, ____, ____

B. What is your place in line . . .

4. if there are two people ahead of you?
5. if there are eight people ahead of you?

C. Finish the sentences about money. Use number words.

6. Three dimes equal ____ cents.
7. One dollar equals one ____ pennies.
8. Five cents and ____ cents equal one quarter.
9. Two quarters equal ____ cents.
10. A quarter, a dime, and a nickel equal ____ cents.

D. Look at the runners in the picture. Write the number words that tell the places of the boys and the girls in the race.

11. boys   12. girls

first
second
third
fourth
fifth
sixth
seventh
eighth
ninth
tenth
twenty
thirty
forty
fifty
hundred

Spelling and Language

NUMBER WORD FAMILIES

Look at the first row of words. See the pattern. Follow the pattern and complete the next four rows.

1. seven   seventh   seventeen   seventy
2. nine   _____   nineteen   ninety
3. three   _____   thirteen   _____
4. four   _____   fourteen   _____
5. five   _____   fifteen   _____

Look at the words in rows **2** through **5**. In each row, what letters do most of the words have in common? Circle the word in each row that doesn't share all of these letters. For example, in row **2** one word doesn't have the u̲.

Proofreading

Kenny sent a package to his cousin. He made three spelling mistakes in the address. He also forgot two capital letters.

1. Find each of Kenny's mistakes.

2. Write the three misspelled words correctly.

3. Now write the address correctly.

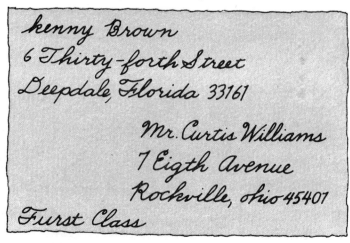

kenny Brown
6 Thirty-forth Street
Deepdale, Florida 33161

     Mr. Curtis Williams
     7 Eigth Avenue
     Rockville, ohio 45407
First Class

Spelling Review

Make believe you are going to the moon. You will be on the moon for ten days. You must report what you do and see every day. Each day's report must tell which day it is — the first day, the second day, and so on. Try to use the words for 20, 30, 40, 50, and 100 in your reports, also.

MASTERY WORDS

Finish these rhymes. Use the Mastery words.

1. One, ____,
   Tie your shoe.

2. Three, ____,
   Shut the door.

3. Five, ____,
   Pick up sticks.

4. Nine, ____,
   Start again.

Finish the riddle. Write the number words.

5. If (2) ____ is company,

6. and (3) ____ is a crowd,

7. what are (4) ____ and five?

8. Answer: (9) ____.

two
three
four
six
nine
ten

BONUS WORDS

Add or multiply. Write the number words.

1. 9 + 10   **2.** 1 + 10   **3.** 10 × 6
4. 10 × 100   **5.** 5 + 10   **6.** 2 + 10
7. 10 × 8   **8.** 3 + 10   **9.** 500 + 500

Follow the directions. Use the Bonus words.
10. Count from 10 to 20. Write the number words.
11. Use each Bonus word in a sentence.

eleven
twelve
thirteen
fifteen
nineteen
sixty
eighty
thousand

107

27 REVIEW

UNIT 19
anyway
bedroom
everybody
maybe
sometimes

UNIT 20
didn't
I'll
let's
there's
won't

Follow these steps as you study each review word.

● Read the word. Name each letter in the word.
● Say the word to yourself. Listen to each sound.
● Copy the word on another piece of paper. Write the word again without looking at your book. Then check what you wrote against the word in your book.
● Practice writing the word until you are <u>sure</u> you know how to spell it.

UNIT 19   Add one of these words to each word below. Write the review words.

times	way	be	room	body

1. may   2. every   3. bed
4. some   5. any

UNIT 20   Write contractions for these words.

6. will not   7. let us
8. did not   9. there is

Start with this sentence.
I will be leaving tomorrow.
10. Rewrite the sentence using a contraction.
11. Write the sentence so it means the opposite. Use another contraction.

UNIT 21   Finish the story. Use the review words. The sounds /ô/ and /ôr/ are given as clues.

My aunt /ô/ **12** us a funny game.
You draw straws. There are /ôr/ **13**
long ones and one /ôr/ **14** one.
Whoever gets the short /ô/ **15**
must /ô/ **16** only in rhyme. I got the
/ôr/ **17** /ô/ **18** . So wherever I walk,
in rhymes I must /ô/ **19** .

UNIT 22   Follow the directions. Use the review words.

20. Write the word that is a compound word.
21. Write the two words that have /ûr/ spelled <u>ear</u>.
22. Write two words and finish the sentence. When will Fern ____ from her trip around the ____ ?

UNIT 23   Follow the directions. Use the review words.

23. Write the three words that have the sounds /är/. Draw a line under the letters that spell /är/.
24. Write the two words that have the sounds /âr/. Draw a line under the letters that spell /âr/.

UNIT 21
talk
taught
straw
short
four

UNIT 22
birthday
heard
learn
return
world

UNIT 23
park
yard
heart
stairs
bear

109

UNIT 24   Write the plurals of these words.

25. puppy   **26.** marble
27. eye   **28.** butterfly

Look at this drawing of a cat.
29. What four things are
    missing?

UNIT 25   Write the words for these
pronunciations.

30. /rōt/   **31.** /nok/   **32.** /klīm/
33. /haf/   **34.** /gōst/

Finish the sentences. Use the review words
from Unit 25.
35. We heard a strange ____ on the attic door.
36. I wanted to ____ up and see what it was.
37. Emma said it was a ____.
38. I was only ____ sure she wasn't right.

UNIT 26   Kelly, Juan, Jane, Sam, and Eriko
are standing in line. Kelly is first. Juan is
second. Eriko is last. Write the words that tell
these children's places in line.

39. Sam   **40.** Jane

Write the words for these numbers.
41. 100   **42.** 20   **43.** 40

Write the underlined words correctly.
44. My friend Chad is in the <u>forth</u> grade.
45. There are <u>twenny</u> people in his class.

110

Writing On Your Own

Marbles are smooth and round. They are bright balls of colored glass. Some marbles have swirls of color. Some marbles look like a cat's eyes.

The picture <u>shows</u> us marbles. The sentences <u>tell</u> us about marbles. The sentences draw a <u>word picture</u> of marbles.

1. Write a sentence about one of the pictures. Your sentence should tell one special thing about the bear or the puppies.
2. Write a word picture to go with one of the pictures. Try to tell as much about the animal as the picture shows.
3. Think about how these animals move. Then write a word picture that tells how the bear moves or how the puppies move. Your word picture should help the reader "see" the animals moving.

28 Words That End with <u>y</u>

1. family
2. hurry
3. body
4. company
5. lady
6. library
7. party
8. penny
9. pony
10. carry
11. copy
12. cry
13. empty
14. marry
15. study

These families are hurrying.

This Week's Words

All of the words this week end with a consonant and <u>y</u>. Some are nouns. Some are verbs.

To make the nouns plural, change <u>y</u> to <u>i</u> and add <u>es</u>.

      family   families

To make the verbs tell about the past, change <u>y</u> to <u>i</u> and add <u>ed</u>.

      hurry   hurried

The <u>y</u> stays when you add <u>ing</u>.

      hurry   hurrying

REMEMBER THIS: There are two r's in <u>library</u>. They come before and after the <u>a</u>. Think of this. In the library you **r**each **a**nd **r**ead.

112

Spelling Practice

A. Write the singular of each plural noun.

1. bodies   **2.** ladies   **3.** ponies   **4.** pennies

B. Write these words without _ed_. Remember to change a letter.

5. emptied   **6.** cried   **7.** studied   **8.** married

C. Add _ing_ to the word in dark print. Finish each sentence.

9. hurry   Melissa is ___ down the street.
10. carry   She is ___ a bag of groceries.

D. Finish the first sentence with _copy_ + _ed_.
Finish the second sentence with _copy_ + _es_.

11. Steve ___ his paper over until it was perfect.
12. He made five ___ before he was done.

E. Finish the sentences. Use this week's words.

13. There are three people in Hamad's
___.

14. Hamad's father works for a
___ that makes bikes.

15. Hamad's mother works in a
___ that has many books.

16. I met them both at Hamad's
birthday ___.

family
hurry
body
company
lady
library
party
penny
pony
carry
copy
cry
empty
marry
study

113

Spelling and Language

family
hurry
body
company
lady
library
party
penny
pony
carry
copy
cry
empty
marry
study

USING VERBS AND PLURAL NOUNS

You add <u>ed</u> to a verb to tell what already happened. You add <u>ing</u> to make a verb that can be used with <u>am</u>, <u>is</u>, <u>are</u>, <u>was</u>, and <u>were</u>.

Add <u>ed</u> or <u>ing</u> to the words in dark print. Write the verbs that finish the sentences.

1. **carry**   Lena ___ ten books in her book bag.
2. **empty**   She ___ the books on her desk.
3. **study**   Lena is ___ about animals that work.

A plural noun names more than one thing.

Write the plurals of the words in dark print.
4. **pony**   Lena read a book about Shetland ___.
5. **body**   They have short, strong ___.
6. **company**   Mining ___ used them to pull carts.

The Dictionary

There are two vowel sounds in <u>pony</u>. So <u>pony</u> has two **syllables.** The pronunciation for <u>pony</u> has this mark: ′ . It is an **accent mark.** It shows which syllable is said with more force.

> **po·ny** /pō′nē/ *n., pl.* **ponies** A very small horse.

Find the accent mark in each pronunciation. Write **1**, **2**, or **3** to show which syllable the mark follows. Then write the word.

1. /emp′tē/   2. /fam′ə·lē/   3. /pen′ē/   4. /kum′pə·nē/

114

Spelling Review

THIS WEEK'S WORDS

1. Write NOUN and VERB at the top of your paper.
2. Write each of this week's words under the right word. The words <u>hurry</u>, <u>copy</u>, and <u>cry</u> can be nouns or verbs. Write them in both lists.
3. Use one noun and one verb together in a sentence. You can make the noun plural. You can add <u>ed</u> or <u>ing</u> to the verb. Here is an example: "The <u>ladies</u> <u>hurried</u> to the bus stop."
4. Use the nouns and verbs to write two more sentences.

MASTERY WORDS

Follow the directions. Use the Mastery words.
1. Write the three words that end with /ī/.
2. Write the three words that end with /ē/.

Write the singular of each plural noun. Remember to change a letter.
3. cities   4. candies   5. skies   6. babies

Write these Mastery words without <u>ed</u>.
7. tried   8. dried

city
try
baby
sky
dry
candy

BONUS WORDS

1. Write the Bonus word that has two <u>p</u>'s. Use it as a noun and as a verb in a sentence.
2. Write the plurals of the four other nouns.
3. Add <u>ed</u> and <u>ing</u> to the three other verbs.
4. Write a story about hidden treasure. Try to use all the Bonus words in your story.

bury
colony
deny
enemy
envy
factory
memory
supply

29 The Sounds /əl/ and /ər/

1. *purple*
2. *camel*
3. *cover*
4. *able*
5. *bottle*
6. *eagle*
7. *people*
8. *table*
9. *level*
10. *nickel*
11. *shovel*
12. *either*
13. *letter*
14. *summer*
15. *sugar*

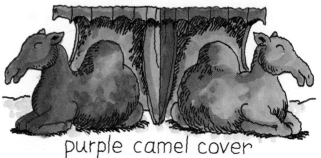

purple camel cover

This Week's Words

All the words this week have two vowel sounds. We say that they have two **syllables.** The first syllable in each word is said with more force. The second syllable has a weak vowel sound called a **schwa.** We use this sign to show the schwa: /ə/.

/əl/ The schwa with /l/ is spelled **le** in <u>purple</u> and **el** in <u>camel</u>.

/ər/ The schwa with /r/ is often spelled **er,** as in <u>cover</u>. But it can be spelled with other vowel letters. It is spelled **ar** in <u>sugar</u>.

REMEMBER THIS: There are two ways to say <u>either</u>. One way begins with long <u>e</u>: /ēʹthər/. The other way begins with long <u>i</u>: /īʹthər/. That's good. It helps us remember to put e and i in <u>either</u>.

116

Spelling Practice

A. Follow the directions. Use this week's words.

1. Write the three words that name things in the picture.
2. Write three more words that have /əl/ spelled the same way.
3. Write the word for this picture.
4. Write three more words that have /əl/ spelled this way.
5. Write the three words that begin with vowel sounds.

B. Add the letters that stand for /ər/. Write the words.

6. cov___
7. lett___
8. eith___
9. sug___
10. summ___

C. Read the clues. Then write the words.

11. I have four legs and a long <u>a</u>.
12. I have a short <u>u</u> and I dig.
13. I have a head on one side and a short <u>i</u>.

purple
camel
cover
able
bottle
eagle
people
table
level
nickel
shovel
either
letter
summer
sugar

117

purple
camel
cover
able
bottle
eagle
people
table
level
nickel
shovel
either
letter
summer
sugar

Spelling and Language

PLURAL NOUNS

A plural noun names more than one thing. You add <u>s</u> to most nouns to make them plural.

Finish the sentences. Use this week's words as plurals.

1. Bald ＿＿ have white feathers on their heads.
2. Some ＿＿ have one hump, others have two.
3. There are seven ＿＿ in the word <u>animals</u>.

Finish this sentence. Use one of this week's words. Then answer the questions.

4. Many ＿＿ visited the zoo today.
5. Does the word you wrote name more than one?
6. Did you have to add <u>s</u> to make the word plural?

Proofreading

Wendy made up a shopping list. She made three spelling mistakes in her list.

1. Read Wendy's list and find each mistake.

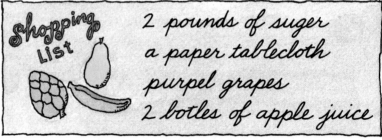

shopping List
2 pounds of suger
a paper tablecloth
purpel grapes
2 botles of apple juice

2. Write the three misspelled words correctly.

118

Spelling Review

THIS WEEK'S WORDS

Here are the first syllables of all of this week's words. Add the missing syllable to each one. Write the whole word.

1. sum   **2.** lev   **3.** bot   **4.** pur   **5.** ea

6. cam   **7.** ta   **8.** cov   **9.** shov   **10.** let

11. ei   **12.** nick   **13.** peo   **14.** a   **15.** sug

MASTERY WORDS

after
dollar
ever
other
over
river

Add the vowel letters. Write the Mastery words.

1. d_ll_r   **2.** _th_r   **3.** r_v_r   **4.** _ft_r

Write the Mastery words that mean the opposite.

5. under   **6.** before   **7.** never

Write Mastery words and finish the sentence.

8. And they lived happily _____ _____.

BONUS WORDS

answer
clever
collar
paddle
polar
puzzle
travel
tunnel

Write the Bonus words that go with these words.

1. jigsaw _____   **2.** _____ fox

3. underground _____   **4.** _____ the phone

5. canoe _____   **6.** _____ bear

7. _____ far   **8.** leash and _____

Use these pairs of Bonus words in sentences.

9. The two words that end with <u>le</u>.

10. The two words that end with <u>el</u>.

11. The two words that end with <u>er</u>.

12. The two words that end with <u>ar</u>.

119

30 Homophones

1. sale
2. sail
3. beat
4. beet
5. break
6. brake
7. main
8. mane
9. read
10. reed
11. meet
12. rode
13. son
14. whose
15. won

This Week's Words

Sale and sail are **homophones.** They sound alike, but they are not spelled alike. They also have different meanings.

Homophones can be tricky. You must pay attention to what the words mean. Then you can write the words that make sense in your sentences.

Spelling Practice

A. Write the homophones for these words. Use this week's words.

1. who's
2. sun
3. road
4. one
5. meat

B. There is a word in each sentence that doesn't make sense. Find that word. Then write the right word.

6. The horse has a long, white main.
7. You step on the break to stop a car.
8. The store is having a sail on jeans.
9. Tim's face is as red as a beat.
10. Gail made a flute out of a read.

C. Finish each sentence. Use the word that has the right meaning.

11. Miko and Chris ___ a book every week.
12. I hope our team can ___ the other team.
13. Children ___ their toy boats on this pond.
14. Dad can ___ open an egg with one hand.
15. What is the ___ street in your town called?

D. Rewrite this sentence. Use <u>road</u> and its homophone.

16. We took a ride down the road.

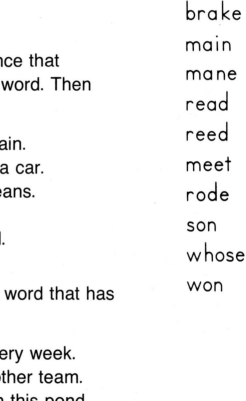

sale
sail
beat
beet
break
brake
main
mane
read
reed
meet
rode
son
whose
won

Spelling and Language

sale
sail
beat
beet
break
brake
main
mane
read
reed
meet
rode
son
whose
won

WHOSE AND WHO'S

You use <u>whose</u> to ask questions about who owns something. "<u>Whose</u> pencil is this?" The word <u>who's</u> is a contraction for <u>who is</u> or <u>who has</u>. You use <u>who's</u> to ask this kind of question: "<u>Who's</u> got my pencil?"

Start each of these questions with <u>Whose</u> or <u>Who's</u>.

1. ＿＿ going to the zoo with you?
2. ＿＿ desk is next to yours?
3. ＿＿ bean plant is taller, yours or mine?
4. ＿＿ taller, Anita or Pedro?
5. ＿＿ been using this paintbrush?

The Dictionary

A **pronunciation** is a special way of writing a word. It shows you how to say the word. As you can see, the pronunciations for <u>who's</u> and <u>whose</u> are the same.

who's /hōoz/ **1** Who is: *Who's* ready for recess? **2** Who has: *Who's* got my notebook?
whose /hōoz/ *pron.* Belonging to which person: *Whose* book is this?

Write the two words for each pronunciation.

1. /brāk/　　　2. /sāl/　　　3. /rēd/
4. /bēt/　　　5. /mān/

122

Spelling Review

Write sentences using homophone pairs. Use this week's words. Use the homophones you know for <u>meet</u>, <u>rode</u>, <u>son</u>, <u>whose</u>, and <u>won</u>, too. Here is an example: "Let's <u>meet</u> at the <u>meat</u> store."

MASTERY WORDS

Follow the directions. Use the Mastery words.
1. Write the word that means "listen." Then write the word that sounds the same.
2. Write the word that names what comes from trees. Then write the word that sounds the same.

Finish the sentences. Use two Mastery words.
3. Pak walks his little brother ____ school.
4. His brother is ____ little to go alone.

here
too
would
to
wood
hear

BONUS WORDS

Some homophones are mixed up in this story. Write the story correctly. Then finish the story.

    The night had groan cold. Nan could smell the cent of pine needles. The wind whistled through a broken pain. It sounded like the grown of someone in pane. Nan thought, "For two scents I'd leave this cabin and go home." But she knew the hole situation would seem better in the morning.
    Suddenly Nan heard a loud cracking sound.

groan
hole
pain
scent
whole
cent
grown
pane

31 The Sounds /o͝o/ and /o͞o/

1. balloon
2. brook
3. shook
4. stood
5. goodness
6. choose
7. noon
8. raccoon
9. roof
10. tooth
11. group
12. soup
13. flew
14. grew
15. lose

This Week's Words

There are two sounds that are spelled with **oo**: /o͝o/, heard in <u>brook</u>, and /o͞o/, heard in <u>noon</u>.

The sound /o͞o/ can also be spelled with these letters.

- **ou,** as in <u>group</u>
- **ew,** as in <u>flew</u>
- ☐ **o,** as in <u>lose</u>

REMEMBER THIS: <u>Choose</u> and <u>lose</u> rhyme, but they are not spelled alike. Don't mix up the spellings. If you spell <u>lose</u> like <u>choose</u>, you get a word that rhymes with <u>goose</u>.

The goose is loose.

Spelling Practice

A. Follow the directions. Use this week's words.

1. Write the four words that have the same vowel sound as <u>look</u>.

2. Write the three words that have double consonant letters.

3. Write the two words that rhyme with <u>new</u>.

4. Write the two words that rhyme but have /o͞o/ spelled in different ways.

5. Write the word that is the same forward and backward.

B. Finish the story. Use this week's words.

One night I dreamed that a dragon __6__ over our house. It landed on the __7__. The whole house __8__ when it landed. A large __9__ of people came to look at the dragon. When it saw all the people, it smiled. It had only one big __10__ in its mouth. The dragon looked hungry. So we fed it some __11__.

balloon
brook
shook
stood
goodness
choose
noon
raccoon
roof
tooth
group
soup
flew
grew
lose

balloon
brook
shook
stood
goodness
choose
noon
raccoon
roof
tooth
group
soup
flew
grew
lose

Spelling and Language

VERBS FOR NOW AND BEFORE

Often you add <u>ed</u> to a verb to talk about what already happened. "Dogs <u>bark</u>. Dogs <u>barked</u>." Sometimes the whole word changes. "Dogs <u>eat</u> meat. Dogs <u>ate</u> meat."

Finish the chart. Use this week's words.

NOW	BEFORE	BEFORE	NOW
eat	**ate**	**saw**	**see**
1. fly	____	5. lost	____
2. shake	____	6. chose	____
3. stand	____		
4. grow	____		

Proofreading

Peter wrote this story about a boy and a balloon. He made six mistakes in spelling.
1. Read the story and find each mistake.

> Once upon a time a little boy had a red balloon. He was afraid he would loose his balloon. So he tied it to his hand. But the string came loose. The balloon floo away. The boy chased it. The baloon flew over a brook. The boy stod and watched it. It greu smaller and smaller.
>
> Two weeks later the boy saw a racoon. The raccoon was carrying something red. It was the lost red balloon!

2. Write the six misspelled words correctly.

Spelling Review

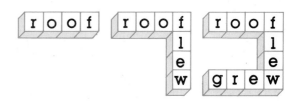

THIS WEEK'S WORDS

Make a "word chain" with this week's words. Write one word. Use a letter in that word to write another word. Then keep going, writing words across and down. Try to link up all the words in one chain. Or you may make more than one chain.

MASTERY WORDS

Follow the directions. Use the Mastery words.
1. Write the two words that have the same vowel sound as <u>book</u>.
2. Write the four words that have the same vowel sound as <u>noon</u>.
3. Write the word that tells when.
4. Write the word that is not spelled with <u>oo</u>.

Write the Mastery words that mean the opposite.
5. old   6. gave

took
room
soon
wool
new
school

BONUS WORDS

1. Write the three words that end with /o͞o/.
2. Write the five words spelled with <u>oo</u>.
3. Write this sentence over. Use three Bonus words that mean the opposite of the underlined words. "The <u>local person</u> drove down a <u>straight</u> but <u>bumpy</u> road."
4. <u>Chew</u> and <u>stew</u> both end with <u>ew</u>. Add other consonants to <u>ew</u>. Spell as many words as you can. Then do the same thing with <u>ook</u>.

chew
crooked
lookout
shampoo
smooth
stew
tourist
wooden

32 The Sounds /ou/ and /oi/

1. _loud_
2. _noise_
3. _cloud_
4. _mouse_
5. _mouth_
6. _sound_
7. _brown_
8. _clown_
9. _crown_
10. _owl_
11. _oil_
12. _point_
13. _voice_
14. _joy_
15. _enjoy_

This Week's Words

The vowel sound /ou/ is heard in <u>loud</u>. This sound is spelled two ways.

● /ou/ is spelled **ou** in <u>loud</u>
● /ou/ is spelled **ow** in <u>brown</u>

The vowel sound /oi/ is heard in <u>noise</u>. This sound is also spelled two ways.

● /oi/ is spelled **oi** in <u>noise</u>
● /oi/ is spelled **oy** at the end of <u>joy</u>

Spelling Practice

A. Follow the directions. Use this week's words.

1. Write the three words that name things in the picture.

2. Write the word for the color of the bird.

3. Write two words that mean about the same thing. Here is a hint. They both name things a horn makes.

4. Write three more words that have /oi/ spelled <u>oi</u>.

5. Write four more words that have /ou/ spelled <u>ou</u>.

6. What should you never use in the library? Write a word with /ou/ and a word with /oi/.

7. Write the word that means about the same thing as <u>happiness</u>. Then add two letters. Spell another one of your words.

B. Change the underlined letter in each word. Write one of this week's words.

8. c<u>l</u>own
9. <u>r</u>ound
10. <u>h</u>ouse
11. <u>s</u>outh

loud
noise
cloud
mouse
mouth
sound
brown
clown
crown
owl
oil
point
voice
joy
enjoy

QUIET
PLEASE

129

loud
noise
cloud
mouse
mouth
sound
brown
clown
crown
owl
oil
point
voice
joy
enjoy

Spelling and Language

PLURAL NOUNS

A plural noun names more than one thing. You add <u>s</u> to most nouns to make them plural.

Finish the sentences. Write the plurals of this week's words. Use each word only once.
1. There were dark ___ in the sky.
2. Ned could hear the ___ of thunder and wind.
3. Ned's brother was afraid of loud ___.
4. Ned said, "Let's open our ___ and sing."
5. "Our ___ will block out the thunder."

The Dictionary

A **definition** tells what a word means. Read the definitions for <u>noise</u> and <u>sound</u>. <u>Noise</u> has just one definition. <u>Sound</u> has more than one.

noise /noiz/ *n.* Sound, especially loud sound: The crowd made a lot of *noise*.

sound /sound/ *n.* Anything that can be heard: Don't make a *sound*!
—*v.* **1** To make a sound: *Sound* the horn. **2** To seem: It *sounds* right to me.

Read each sentence. Can <u>noise</u> take the place of <u>sound</u>? If it can, write <u>noise</u> or <u>noises</u>.
1. The story <u>sounds</u> exciting.
2. The cat was making angry <u>sounds</u>.
3. Shall I <u>sound</u> the dinner bell?
4. Julie heard a banging <u>sound</u> outside.

Spelling Review

THIS WEEK'S WORDS

Add the letters that spell /ou/. Write the words.
1. cl__d   2. cr__n   3. m__th   4. __l
5. br__n   6. m__se   7. l__d   8. s__nd
9. cl__n

Add the letters that spell /oi/. Write the words.
10. n__se   11. __l   12. enj__   13. p__nt
14. v__ce   15. j__

MASTERY WORDS

Follow the directions. Use the Mastery words.
1. Write the word that starts with /ou/.
2. Write the two words that have <u>out</u> in them.

Write Mastery words that rhyme with these words.
3. sound   4. down   5. mouse   6. out

Write the Mastery words that mean the opposite.
7. whisper   8. lost

about
found
house
our
shout
town

BONUS WORDS

Follow the directions. Use the Bonus words.
1. Write the four words that have the sound /ou/.
2. Write the four words that have the sound /oi/.
3. Write the two verbs that mean "wreck, or ruin."

Add <u>ed</u> to each of these words. Then use the words with <u>ed</u> in sentences.
4. spoil   5. destroy   6. bounce   7. frown

spoil
coins
loyal
destroy
bounce
proud
frown
towel

33 Words with <u>ou</u> and <u>ough</u>

1. double
2. country
3. cousin
4. touch
5. count
6. flour
7. round
8. bought
9. brought
10. thought
11. although
12. though
13. tough
14. rough
15. enough

This Week's Words

In <u>double</u>, <u>country</u>, <u>cousin</u>, and <u>touch</u>,
The <u>o-u</u> sounds like the <u>u</u> in <u>much</u>.

In <u>count</u> and <u>flour</u> and also in <u>round</u>,
The <u>o-u</u> has a howling sound.

With <u>g-h</u> in <u>bought</u>, <u>brought</u>, and <u>thought</u>,
The <u>o-u</u> sounds like the end of <u>paw</u>.

The <u>o-u-g-h</u> in <u>although</u> and <u>though</u>
Sounds surprised—scared of a shadow.

These same four letters huff and puff
In <u>tough</u> and <u>rough</u> and in <u>enough</u>.

Spelling Practice

A. Follow the directions. Use this week's words.

1. Write a word that means "hard to chew." (It rhymes with <u>stuff</u>.)
2. Add an <u>h</u> to make a word that means "even if." (It rhymes with <u>go</u>.)
3. Add a <u>t</u> to make a word that means "did think." (It rhymes with <u>caught</u>.)

4. Write the three words that end with the sound /f/.

5. Write four more words that have the sound /u/ as in <u>up</u>.

6. Write the two words that end with /ō/.

7. Write the three words that have the sound /ou/.

8. Write the three words that rhyme with <u>caught</u>.

B. Use this week's words to finish these questions and answers.

9. Did she buy her friend a tie?
   Yes, she ____ her friend a tie.

10. Did she bring it to his birthday party?
    Yes, she ____ it to his birthday party.

11. Did he think the tie was nice?
    Yes, he ____ the tie was nice.

double
country
cousin
touch
count
flour
round
bought
brought
thought
although
though
tough
rough
enough

Spelling and Language

double
country
cousin
touch
count
flour
round
bought
brought
thought
although
though
tough
rough
enough

RHYMING WORDS

Finish the poem with this week's words. The words must rhyme with the words in dark print.

Come to my house in about an **hour,**
And help me make bread from yeast and __1__.
First we mix and knead the **dough**
Until it's smooth. But __2__
We must be sure to knead it **enough,**
If we do it too much, the bread will be __3__.
Then after all the kneading and **trouble,**
We leave it to rise until it is __4__.
After we bake it just as we **ought,**
We'll have fresh bread—quicker than you __5__.

Proofreading

Diane wrote down this phone message for her mother. She made six spelling mistakes.

1. Read the message and find each mistake.

Mrs. Logan called at 3:00. She visited her cosin in the contry. She broght back enuff fresh corn for everybody. We can cont on having some for dinner. Please get in tuch with her.

2. Write the six misspelled words correctly.

134

Spelling Review

Use all the words to make a word search puzzle. You can write the words across or down. Fill in the empty spaces with other letters. Then let someone else solve it.

C	A	C	R	O	F	E
G	D	O	U	B	L	E
C	O	U	S	I	N	M
R	E	N	N	I	E	A
R	K	T	O	U	G	H

MASTERY WORDS

Follow the directions. Use the Mastery words.
1. Write the four words with /ō/ as in <u>low</u>.
2. Write the three words with /ou/ as in <u>cow</u>.
3. Write the word you wrote for both **1** and **2**.

Use one Mastery word to finish both sentences.
4. Take the oars and ____ the boat.
5. Tall people must stand in the back ____.

> **row**
> **slow**
> **yellow**
> **bow**
> **how**
> **tower**

BONUS WORDS

Write the two words in each group that have the same vowel sound.

1. couple	2. cough	3. trousers	4. shoulder
cup	tough	trouble	cold
soup	off	houses	should

Finish these sentences with Bonus words.
5. <u>Think</u> is to <u>thought</u> as <u>fight</u> is to ____.
6. <u>North</u> is to <u>northern</u> as <u>south</u> is to ____.

Write sentences using the Bonus words. Try to use two Bonus words in each sentence.

> **couple**
> **southern**
> **south**
> **county**
> **trousers**
> **cough**
> **fought**
> **shoulder**

34 Syllable Patterns

1. *butter*
2. *cattle*
3. *dinner*
4. *funny*
5. *happen*
6. *lesson*
7. *matter*
8. *middle*
9. *rabbit*
10. *corner*
11. *forgot*
12. *number*
13. *perhaps*
14. *problem*
15. *wonder*

This Week's Words

All the words this week have two vowel sounds. We say that they have two **syllables.**

Some of the words have double consonant letters in the middle: but_ter. These words are divided into syllables between the double consonant letters.

Some of the words have two different consonant letters in the middle: cor_ner. These words are divided into syllables between those consonant letters.

Spelling Practice

A. Write this week's words that have these double consonant letters. Then draw a line between the two syllables.

1. bb
2. ss
3. pp
4. nn (two words)
5. tt (three words)

6. Now write the word that tells where you divided the words.

B. Add one of the syllables in the box to one of the numbered syllables. Write some of this week's words.

lem	ner	der	got	ber	haps

7. num
8. prob
9. per
10. cor
11. for
12. won

C. Copy these words. Write one of this week's words that rhymes with each word. Then draw a line between the two syllables in each pair.

13. winner
14. batter
15. sunny
16. riddle
17. mutter
18. battle

butter
cattle
dinner
funny
happen
lesson
matter
middle
rabbit
corner
forgot
number
perhaps
problem
wonder

137

| butter |
| cattle |
| dinner |
| funny |
| happen |
| lesson |
| matter |
| middle |
| rabbit |
| corner |
| forgot |
| number |
| perhaps |
| problem |
| wonder |

Spelling and Language

NOUNS AND VERBS

A **noun** names a person, a place, or a thing. A **verb** shows action or being. Finish each pair of sentences with one of this week's words. The word will be a noun in the first sentence and a verb in the second.

1. Do you want jam or just ___ on your toast?
2. I will ___ it for you, if you'd like.
3. Do you know what's the ___ with Abigail?
4. Does it ___ to you that she's sad?
5. Wally and Nava chased the dog around the ___ .
6. Finally they were able to ___ him.
7. Start with the ___ 1.
8. Then ___ your paper from 1 to 25.

The Dictionary

The pronunciation for a two-syllable word has an accent mark. It shows which syllable is said with more force. The first syllable in <u>butter</u> is the accented syllable.

but·ter /but′ər/

Write the words that go with the pronunciations. Then draw a line under the letters in the accented syllable.

1. /prob′ləm/   2. /mid′əl/   3. /pər·haps′/
4. /fər·got′/   5. /les′ən/   6. /wun′dər/

138

Spelling Review

Write some funny story titles. Use this week's words. Try to use more than one of the words in each title. Here are some examples: "The Rabbit Who Forgot How to Hop" and "The Mad Hatter's Funny Dinner."

MASTERY WORDS

Follow the directions. Use the Mastery words.
1. Write the two words that have double l.
2. Write these two words again. Draw a line under the letters that spell /ō/.

Add the letters that spell the second syllable of each word. Write the whole word.

3. sis   **4.** sun   **5.** hap

6. pret   **7.** hel   **8.** fol

follow
happy
hello
pretty
sunny
sister

BONUS WORDS

1. Write all the Bonus words in alphabetical order. Then draw a line between the two syllables in each word.
2. Write the three words that are spelled with double l. Then circle the word that ends with the vowel sound in cow.
3. Use swallow and tonsils in a sentence.
4. Write sentences using the words welcome, practice, and swallow as nouns. Then write sentences using each word as a verb.

stammer
swallow
hollow
allow
tonsils
seldom
welcome
practice

35 Another Syllable Pattern

1. *pilot*
2. *above*
3. *ahead*
4. *alike*
5. *alone*
6. *around*
7. *become*
8. *begin*
9. *behind*
10. *belong*
11. *below*
12. *beside*
13. *motor*
14. *paper*
15. *parade*

This Week's Words

All the words this week have two syllables. Each word has one consonant letter between the two vowel sounds.

All of this week's words are divided into syllables before the consonant.

Spelling Practice

A. Add <u>a</u> or <u>be</u> to these words. Write this week's words.

1. come
2. side
3. head
4. low
5. round
6. like

B. Follow the directions. Use this week's words.

7. Add one of the syllables in the circle to each of the syllables in the box. Write five words.

a
be

gin	long	hind
	bove	lone

8. Write the four words that do not have <u>a</u> or <u>be</u> as the first syllable. Draw a line between the two syllables in each word.

9. Write two pairs of words that are opposites. One word in each pair has the first syllable <u>a</u>. The other one has the first syllable <u>be</u>.

C. The accented syllable is the one you say with more force. Write the words that have these accented syllables.

10. pi
11. mo
12. rade
13. pa

pilot
above
ahead
alike
alone
around
become
begin
behind
belong
below
beside
motor
paper
parade

141

Spelling and Language

WORDS FOR WHERE AND HOW

pilot
above
ahead
alike
alone
around
become
begin
behind
belong
below
beside
motor
paper
parade

Many of this week's words tell where or how. Look at these shapes. Then finish the sentences about them. Use this week's words.

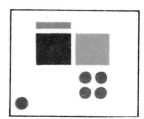

1. The purple square is ＿＿ the green square.
2. The orange line is ＿＿ the purple square.
3. The red dots are ＿＿ the green square.
4. The four red dots are all ＿＿.
5. The blue dot is ＿＿ in the corner.
6. A black line is ＿＿ all the shapes.

Proofreading

1. There are six spelling mistakes in Theo's sign. Read the sign and find each one.

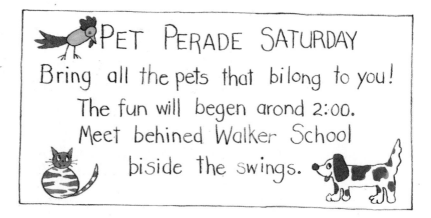

PET PERADE SATURDAY
Bring all the pets that bilong to you!
The fun will begen arond 2:00.
Meet behined Walker School
biside the swings.

2. Write the six misspelled words correctly.

Spelling Review

THIS WEEK'S WORDS

First, write the words that go with the pronunciations.

1. /pā′pər/   **2.** /bi·gin′/   **3.** /pə·rād′/   **4.** /bi·lông′/
5. /pī′lət/   **6.** /bi·kum′/   **7.** /mō′tər/

Now write the other eight words. Then look around your classroom. Use each of these eight words in sentences. Tell about what you see. Here is an example: "The clock is <u>above</u> the chalkboard."

MASTERY WORDS

Follow the directions. Use the Mastery words.
1. Write the word you use to tell why.
2. Write the word that has the sound /ī/.
3. Write the word with the letters <u>ai</u> but not the sound /ā/.

Add <u>a</u> to each word. Write Mastery words.
4. go   **5.** wake   **6.** way   **7.** gain

again
ago
awake
away
because
tiger

BONUS WORDS

1. Write all the Bonus words. Then draw a line to divide each word into syllables.
2. You say the second syllable of three of the words with more force. Write these words.
3. Write the six words that have a long vowel sound in the first syllable.
4. Write the four words that have /əl/ or /ən/.
5. Write sentences using all the Bonus words.

broken
final
machine
motel
pretend
reason
spider
total

143

36 REVIEW

Follow these steps as you study each review word.

- Read the word. Name each letter in the word.
- Say the word to yourself. Listen to each sound.
- Copy the word on another piece of paper. Write the word again without looking at your book. Then check what you wrote against the word in your book.
- Practice writing the word until you are <u>sure</u> you know how to spell it.

UNIT 28   Write the singular of each plural noun.

1. families   **2.** libraries

Write these words without <u>ed</u>. Remember to change a letter.

3. studied   **4.** hurried   **5.** emptied

Add <u>ing</u> to a word from Unit 28. Finish each sentence.

6. Leah is ___ for a spelling test.
7. Buddy is ___ the sand from his shoes.

UNIT 29   Follow the directions. Use the review words.

8. Write the three words that end with /ər/.
9. Write the two words that end with /əl/.
10. Write the two words that have /ē/.

144

UNIT 30   Write the homophone for each of these words.

11. sail **12.** road **13.** who's
14. brake **15.** reed

Find the word in each sentence that doesn't make sense. Then write the right word.
16. Reggie can reed a road map.
17. Who's going to the bake sail?
18. How did you brake your arm?

UNIT 31   Follow the directions. Use the review words.

19. Write the three words spelled with <u>oo</u>. Circle the one with the vowel sound heard in <u>book</u>.
20. Write the word that sounds like <u>chews</u>.
21. Write the word that rhymes with <u>you</u>.

Add the letters that stand for /ōō/. Write the words.
22. gr__p **23.** gr__

UNIT 32   Follow the directions. Use the review words.

24. Write the three words with the vowel sound heard in <u>out</u>.
25. Write the two words with the vowel sound heard in <u>toy</u>.
26. Add a letter to the word in dark print. Answer the riddle.
What is a sneeze?   A **nose** ____ .

UNIT 30
break
read
rode
sale
whose

UNIT 31
choose
noon
group
grew
stood

UNIT 32
brown
enjoy
loud
mouth
noise

145

UNIT 33   Write the words for these pronunciations.

27. /thō/   **28.** /kun'trē/   **29.** /i·nuf'/

Write the words that rhyme with these words.
30. sound   **31.** dough
32. bought   **33.** rough

UNIT 34   Write the words that have these vowel sounds. The sounds are given in the right order.

34. /a/, /ə/   **35.** /e/, /ə/   **36.** /o/, /ə/
37. /u/, /ə/   **38.** /ə/, /a/

Follow the directions. Use the words from Unit 34.
39. Write the word for something you solve.
40. Write the word that means "maybe."

UNIT 35   These letters spell the first syllables of four review words. Write the words.

41. be   **42.** pa

Finish the sentences. Use the words from Unit 35.
43. There's going to be a ___ on Saturday.
44. I read all about it in the ___.
45. It's going to ___ at noon.
46. Let's try to get there ___ of time.
47. Then we won't have to stand ___ any tall people.

146

Writing On Your Own

Write about the picture.

1. Write two or three sentences about the children in the picture. What are they doing? Are they having a good time?
2. Pretend that you are sliding down the sand pile. Tell what it feels like. Does the sand feel warm and dry or cool and damp? Does the sand get into your socks? Does the wind blow on your face?
3. Pretend that you had spent the whole day playing with the children in the picture. What other things might you have done? Make believe that you are writing about the day in your diary. Tell about everything that happened that day.

Spelling Dictionary

A

a·ble /ā′bəl/ *adj.* Having the skill: Jane is *able* to swim.

a·bout /ə·bout′/ *prep.* Having to do with: This story is *about* cats.
—*adv.* Almost: Are you just *about* ready?

a·bove /ə·buv′/ *prep.* Over: Paul hung the picture *above* his desk.

a·corn /ā′kôrn/ *n.* Seed of an oak tree.

act /akt/ *v.* **1** To do something. **2** To behave in a certain way: Don't *act* silly. **3** To play a part: Tina will *act* in the play.

—*n.* **1** Something done: Feeding birds is a kind *act.* **2** Part of a play: The third *act* was funny.

add /ad/ *v.* To put two or more numbers or things together.

a·dult /ə·dult′ *or* ad′ult/ *n.* A grown-up person.

af·ter /af′tər/ *prep.* **1** Later than: We got home *after* dark. **2** Following: Friday comes *after* Thursday.

af·ter·noon /af′tər·nōōn′/ *n.* The time between noon and sunset.

a·gain /ə·gen′/ *adv.* Once more.

age /āj/ *n.* **1** The time someone or something has lived: Robin and Tom are the same *age.* **2** A period of time in history: We live in the space *age.*
—*v.* **aged, aging** To grow old.

a·go /ə·gō′/ *adj., adv.* In the past: I got my dog a year *ago.*

a·head /ə·hed′/ *adv.* In front; before: Miguel was *ahead* of me in line.

air /âr/ *n.* **1** What we breathe. **2** The sky: up in the *air.*
—*v.* To let air in: Open the window and *air* out the room.

a·larm /ə·lärm′/ *n.* A signal that warns of danger: fire *alarm.*
—*v.* To frighten: Loud noises *alarm* me.

a·like /ə·līk′/ *adj.* The same.

al·low /ə·lou′/ *v.* To permit: Dogs are not *allowed* on the beach.

a·lone /ə·lōn′/ *adj.* Without anyone or anything near.
—*adv.* Without help: Julia baked the cake *alone.*

al·so /ôl′sō/ *adv.* Too: Raymond *also* plays baseball.

al·though /ôl·thō′/ *conj.* Even if: *Although* I'm busy, I'll help you.

and /and/ *conj.* Also; added to.

an·gry /ang′grē/ *adj.* **angrier, angriest** Feeling anger; mad: The *angry* dog growled.

an·oth·er /ə·nuth′ər/ *adj.* **1** One more: May I have *another* apple? **2** A different one: Kurt moved to *another* city.

an·swer /an′sər/ *n.* **1** A reply. **2** A way of solving a problem: What is the *answer* to the riddle?
—*v.* To reply.

ant /ant/ *n.* A small crawling insect.

an·y /en′ē/ *adj.* No special one: *Any* coat will do.

an·y·one /en′i·wun′/ *pron.* No special person: *Anyone* can come.

an·y·thing /en′i·thing′/ *pron.* No special thing: I'll eat *anything.*

an·y·way /en′i·wā′/ *adv.* Anyhow: If it rains, we'll go *anyway.*

ap·ple /ap′əl/ *n.* A round fruit with a thin red, yellow, or green skin.

aren't /ärnt/ Are not.

ar·gue /är′gyōō/ *v.* **argued, arguing** **1** To disagree. **2** To give reasons for or against: Jim *argued* against skipping recess.

---

n. = **noun**, a naming word;   v. = **verb**, an action word;   adj. = **adjective**, a describing word;
adv. = **adverb**, a word that tells when, where, or how;   prep. = **preposition**, such as *from, by, with;*
conj. = **conjunction**, such as *and, but, because;*
interj. = **interjection**, such as *hello, oh.*

arm /ärm/ *n.* **1** The part of your body between your shoulder and hand. **2** A part of a chair.

a·round /ə·round′/ *adv.* Nearby: The cat is *around* here somewhere. —*prep.* On all sides: There is a fence *around* the house.

art /ärt/ *n.* **1** Drawing, painting, or making statues: Ms. Fong teaches *art.* **2** Great paintings or statues.

ar·tist /är′tist/ *n.* A person who draws, paints, or makes statues.

ask /ask/ *v.* To put a question to.

a·sleep /ə·slēp′/ *adj.* **1** Not awake. **2** Numb: My foot is *asleep.*

a·wake /ə·wāk′/ *adj.* Not sleeping.

a·way /ə·wā′/ *adj.* **1** At a distance: My school is a mile *away.* **2** In a different place: My parents are *away* from home.

a·while /ə·(h)wīl′/ *adv.* For a short time.

B

ba·by /bā′bē/ *n., pl.* **babies** A very young child. —*v.* **babied, babying** To treat gently: My brothers *baby* me.

back /bak/ *n.* The rear part of anything: the *back* of the room. —*v.* To cause to go backward: *Back* the car into the garage. —*adv.* **1** To the rear: Sit *back* in your chair. **2** In or to the place you came from: Go *back* home.

bake /bāk/ *v.* **baked, baking** To cook in an oven.

bal·loon /bə·lōōn′/ *n.* **1** A large bag filled with a gas: They floated over the sea in a *balloon.* **2** A small rubber sack filled with air; a toy: We blew up *balloons* for the party.

band·age /ban′dij/ *n.* Something you put over a cut or sore. —*v.* **bandaged, bandaging** To put on a bandage.

bar·ber /bär′bər/ *n.* A person who cuts hair.

bark¹ /bärk/ *n.* The sound a dog makes. —*v.* To make a sound like a dog.

bark² /bärk/ *n.* The outside covering of a tree.

barn /bärn/ *n.* A farm building.

bat¹ /bat/ *n.* A stick or club used for hitting balls. —*v.* **batted, batting** **1** To hit with a bat. **2** To hit as if with a bat: The child *batted* the doll.

bat² /bat/ *n.* A mouselike animal with wings that flies at night.

beach /bēch/ *n., pl.* **beaches** The sandy shore of an ocean or lake.

bear /bâr/ *n.* A furry wild animal.

beat /bēt/ *v.* **1** To hit over and over: *beat* a drum. **2** To win a game. **3** To stir quickly: *Beat* the eggs. —*n.* The accent in music: That song has a good *beat.*

be·cause /bi·kôz′/ *conj.* For the reason that: We stayed home *because* it was snowing.

be·come /bi·kum′/ *v.* To grow to be: You *become* a teenager at thirteen.

bed·room /bed′rōōm′/ *n.* A room for sleeping.

beet /bēt/ *n.* A red root vegetable.

be·fore /bi·fôr'/ *prep.* Coming ahead of: We took a walk *before* dinner. Alberto came *before* Loni in line.
—*adv.* In the time that is over: Heidi never rode a horse *before*.

be·gin /bi·gin'/ *v.* **began, begun, beginning** To start: School *begins* in September.

be·have /bi·hāv'/ *v.* **behaved, behaving** 1 To act: The children *behaved* like grown-ups. 2 To act properly: Please *behave* yourself.

be·hind /bi·hīnd'/ *prep.* In back of: Kiyo hid *behind* a chair.
—*adv.* In, at, or to the back: Luke stayed *behind* to finish his work.

be·long /bi·lông'/ *v.* 1 To be in the right place: Your hat *belongs* on your head. 2 To be someone's: This pencil *belongs* to Luis. 3 To be one of: I *belong* to a club.

be·low /bi·lō'/ *prep.* Lower than or under: A j goes *below* the line.

bend /bend/ *v.* **bent, bending** 1 To make something curve: June *bent* the clay into a C. 2 To stoop: *Bend* down to pick up the dime.

be·side /bi·sīd'/ *prep.* Next to: Ryan's bed is *beside* the wall.

be·tween /bi·twēn'/ *prep.* In the space dividing two things: Kim sat *between* Alice and Todd. Don't eat *between* meals.

bi·cy·cle /bī'sik·əl/ *n.* A vehicle with two wheels, pedals, and handle-bars.

bike /bīk/ *n.* Short for *bicycle*.

bird /bûrd/ *n.* An animal with two wings and feathers that flies.

birth·day /bûrth'dā'/ *n.* The day you were born.

bite /bīt/ *v.* **bit, bitten** *or* **bit, biting** To cut with the teeth: Barbara *bit* into the apple.
—*n.* 1 A small bit of food: Rita wants a *bite* of your pear. 2 A wound or sting gotten by biting.

blast /blast/ *n.* A loud noise: The horn made a loud *blast*.
—*v.* To make a loud noise: The radio was *blasting*.

blend /blend/ *v.* To mix.

blow¹ /blō/ *v.* **blew, blown, blowing** 1 To move with force: The wind is *blowing*. 2 To push by blowing: The wind *blows* leaves around. 3 To send air out: *Blow* out the candles. 4 To make a sound by blowing: *Blow* your horn. 5 To clear by blowing: I *blew* my nose.

blow² /blō/ *n.* A hard hit.

blue·ber·ry /bloo'ber'ē/ *n., pl.* **blueberries** A round bluish berry.

blue·bird /bloo'bûrd'/ *n.* A small bird with a blue back and wings.

boast /bōst/ *v.* To speak with too much pride; to brag: Jim *boasted* about winning the race.

bod·y /bod'ē/ *n., pl.* **bodies** 1 All of a person or animal: Good food is needed for a healthy *body*. 2 A whole part: a *body* of water.

born /bôrn/ *v.* Brought into the world: Joel was *born* in May.

both /bōth/ *adj., pron.* Two together: *Both* dogs ran. Then *both* stopped.

bot·tle /bot'(ə)l/ *n.* A narrow jar with a small opening at the top.

bought /bôt/ *v.* Past tense of *buy*.

---

act, āte, câre, ärt;   egg, ēven;   if, īce;   on, ōver, ôr;   book, food;   up, tûrn;
ə = a in *ago*, e in *listen*, i in *giraffe*, o in *pilot*, u in *circus*;   yoo = u in *music*;   oil;   out;
chair; sing; shop; thank; that; zh in *treasure*.

bounce /bouns/ *v.* **bounced, bouncing** **1** To hit and spring back: The ball *bounced* off the wall. **2** To cause to bounce: Debra *bounced* the ball.

bow¹ /bou/ *v.* To bend your head or body forward.
—*n.* The act of bowing.

bow² /bō/ *n.* **1** A knot with loops: Tie the ribbon in a *bow*. **2** A thing used for shooting arrows.

brake /brāk/ *n.* What you use to stop a car or bicycle.

branch /branch/ *n., pl.* **branches** An armlike part of a tree.

brave /brāv/ *adj.* Not afraid.

break /brāk/ *v.* **broke, broken, breaking** To crack into pieces.
—*n.* A rest period: The workers took a ten-minute *break*.

bridge /brij/ *n.* Something built over a river or valley to allow people to get to the other side.

bright /brīt/ *adj.* **1** Giving off a lot of light: *bright* sun. **2** Cheerful: a *bright* smile. **3** Smart; clever.

bring /bring/ *v.* **brought, bringing** To carry to or to take along: I will *bring* Lee to the picnic.

bro·ken /brō′kən/ *v.* Past participle of *break*.
—*adj.* **1** Cracked in pieces: Sweep up the *broken* glass. **2** Not working: Our TV set is *broken*.

brook /brŏŏk/ *n.* A small stream.

brought /brôt/ *v.* Past tense of *bring*.

brown /broun/ *n., adj.* The color of chocolate.

bud·dy /bud′ē/ *n., pl.* **buddies** A close friend.

build /bild/ *v.* **built, building** To put pieces together; to make: Rhonda *built* a model airplane.

bump /bump/ *v.* To knock against: Geraldo *bumped* his head.
—*n.* **1** A swelling caused by bumping. **2** An uneven part: The car hit a *bump* in the road.

burn /bûrn/ *v.* **1** To be on fire. **2** To destroy by fire. **3** To hurt with fire or heat: He *burned* his hand.
—*n.* A wound caused by heat.

burst /bûrst/ *v.* **burst, bursting** **1** To break apart suddenly: The balloon *burst*. **2** To break out: We all *burst* into laughter.
—*n.* Something sudden: Kyle won with a *burst* of speed.

bur·y /ber′ē/ *v.* **buried, burying** **1** To put into the ground. **2** To hide or cover up: Kent *buried* his face in the pillow.

bush /bŏŏsh/ *n., pl.* **bushes** A small treelike plant.

bus·y /biz′ē/ *adj.* **1** Doing things: I'm *busy* making lunch. **2** Full of things to do: I had a *busy* day.

but·ter /but′ər/ *n.* A yellow spread for bread made from cream.
—*v.* To spread butter on.

but·ter·fly /but′ər·flī′/ *n., pl.* **butterflies** An insect with four bright-colored wings.

buy /bī/ *v.* **bought, buying** To pay money and get something.
—*n.* Something you get for a low price: A pen for a dime is a *buy*.

c

cab·in /kab′in/ *n.* A small house made of wood.

cage /kāj/ *n.* A box or roomlike place made of wire or iron bars: Clean the bird *cage*.

calf /kaf/ *n., pl.* **calves** A young cow.

cam·el /kam′əl/ *n.* An animal with one or two humps on its back.

cam·er·a /kam′(ə·)rə/ *n.* A small machine used for taking pictures.

camp /kamp/ *n.* A place where people go for vacations: Helen went to summer *camp*.
—*v.* To stay outdoors in a tent or trailer: We *camped* by a pond.

can·dy /kan′dē/ *n., pl.* **candies** A sweet food made with sugar.

cane /kān/ *n.* **1** A stick people use to help them walk. **2** The woody stem of a plant.

can·not /kan′ot *or* ka·not′/ Can not.

can't /kant/ Can not.

card /kärd/ *n.* **1** A piece of stiff paper: a birthday *card*. **2** A card used for playing a game.

care /kâr/ *v.* **cared, caring** **1** To show interest or concern: Mabel *cares* about doing well. **2** To want or like: Would you *care* to come?

car·ry /kar′ē/ *v.* **carried, carrying** To take from one place to another: Flora *carried* her books to school.

cart·wheel /kärt′(h)wēl′/ *n.* Turning sideways to stand on your hands and then on your feet again.

cat /kat/ *n.* A small furry animal.

catch /kach/ *v.* **caught, catching** **1** To get hold of: *Catch* the ball. **2** To trap: The spider *caught* a fly. **3** To discover or find: Mom *caught* me eating in bed. **4** To get an illness: Eric *caught* a cold.

cat·tle /kat′(ə)l/ *n. pl.* Cows, bulls, and steers.

cause /kôz/ *n.* A person or thing that makes something happen; reason: He was the *cause* of the trouble.
—*v.* **caused, causing** To make something happen: A traffic jam *caused* us to be late.

cent /sent/ *n.* A penny.

cer·tain /sûr′tən/ *adj.* **1** Entirely sure: I'm *certain* that I'm right. **2** Not just any: a *certain* one.

chair /châr/ *n.* A seat with a back.

chalk /chôk/ *n.* A powdery stick for writing on the board.

chance /chans/ *n.* **1** What may happen: There's a *chance* of rain. **2** A good time to do something: Amos has a *chance* to go to camp. **3** A risk: I never take *chances*.

chase /chās/ *v.* **chased, chasing** **1** To run after. **2** To drive away: Lucy *chased* the dog away.

cheek /chēk/ *n.* Either side of your face, below your eyes.

cher·ry /cher′ē/ *n., pl.* **cherries** A small, round red fruit with a pit.

chew /chōō/ *v.* To grind up with your teeth: Always *chew* your food well.

child /chīld/ *n., pl.* **children** A young boy or girl.

chin /chin/ *n.* The part of your face below your mouth.

---

act, āte, câre, ärt;   egg, ēven;   if, īce;   on, ōver, ôr;   bŏŏk, fōōd;   up, tûrn;
ə = a in *ago*, e in *listen*, i in *giraffe*, o in *pilot*, u in *circus*;   yōō = u in *music*;   oil;   out;
chair;   sing;   shop;   thank;   that;   zh in *treasure*.

choose /cho͞oz/ *v.* **chose, chosen, choosing** **1** To pick out. **2** To decide to do something: Ronald *chose* to go by himself.

chop /chop/ *v.* **chopped, chopping** **1** To cut with an ax: *Chop* down the tree. **2** To cut into small pieces: Ann is *chopping* onions.

church /chûrch/ *n., pl.* **churches** A building where people worship.

cir·cle /sûr′kəl/ *n.* A round shape. —*v.* **circled, circling** **1** To draw a circle around. **2** To move in a circle: The plane *circled* the field.

cir·cus /sûr′kəs/ *n., pl.* **circuses** A show with animals and clowns.

cit·y /sit′ē/ *n., pl.* **cities** A large town.

clap /klap/ *v.* **clapped, clapping** To hit your hands together. —*n.* A loud noise: We heard the *clap* of thunder.

class /klas/ *n., pl.* **classes** **1** A group of students. **2** People or things that are alike in some way: the middle *class*.

clay /klā/ *n.* **1** Mud that is used to make dishes. **2** Something like dough, used for modeling.

clear /klir/ *adj.* **1** Easy to see through. **2** Not cloudy or foggy: a *clear* sky. **3** Easy to understand. —*adv.* **1** In a clear way: I can hear you loud and *clear*. **2** All the way: *clear* across the room. —*v.* To take things away: Tomas *cleared* the table.

clev·er /klev′ər/ *adj.* **1** Showing skill: a *clever* idea. **2** Very smart: Seth is a *clever* child.

cliff /klif/ *n.* A high, steep rock.

climb /klīm/ *v.* **1** To go up: Ella *climbed* the stairs. **2** To go down, over, or into: Jason *climbed* into the car. —*n.* The act of climbing: It is a long *climb* up the mountain.

close[1] /klōz/ *v.* **closed, closing** **1** To shut: Please *close* the door. **2** To end: Erin *closed* her speech with a poem.

close[2] /klōs/ *adj.* **closer, closest** **1** Near. **2** Almost equal: a *close* race. —*adv.* **closer, closest** Near: Alan sat *close* to the window.

cloth·ing /klō′thing/ *n.* The things you wear.

cloud /kloud/ *n.* **1** A mass of tiny water drops that float in the sky. **2** Anything like a cloud: The car raised a *cloud* of dust.

clown /kloun/ *n.* A person in a circus who makes people laugh. —*v.* To act like a clown.

club /klub/ *n.* **1** A heavy stick. **2** A stick used to hit a ball: a golf *club*. **3** A group of people who join together: a book *club*.

coin /koin/ *n.* A piece of metal used as money.

cold /kōld/ *adj.* **1** Low in temperature. **2** Feeling cold: The children were *cold* and tired. —*n.* **1** A lack of heat: The *cold* made my face sting. **2** A sickness that makes you sneeze and cough.

col·lar /kol′ər/ *n.* **1** A fold of cloth that goes around your neck: The dress has a lace *collar*. **2** A band put on an animal's neck.

col·o·ny /kol′ə·nē/ *n., pl.* **colonies** **1** A group of people who settle in a new country: The first *colony* in America was in Virginia. **2** Ants living and working together.

com·pa·ny /kum′pə·nē/ *n., pl.*
companies **1** Guests: We are
having *company* for dinner. **2** A
business.

cop·y /kop′ē/ *n., pl.* **copies** **1** One
thing that looks just like another.
2 One of many things made at one
time: I have a *copy* of that book.
—*v.* **copied, copying** **1** To make
a copy. **2** To act like someone
else: Delia *copies* everything I do.

corn /kôrn/ *n.* A yellow grain that
grows on the ears of a tall plant.

cor·ner /kôr′nər/ *n.* Where two
walls, streets, or sides meet.
—*v.* To force into a corner; to trap:
The cat *cornered* the mouse.

cor·ral /kə·ral′/ *n.* A fenced-in place
where animals are kept.

cost /kôst/ *n.* The amount someone
charges or pays for something.
—*v.* **cost, costing** To have as its
price: The toy *costs* a dollar.

cough /kôf/ *v.* To push air out with a
sudden noise.
—*n.* The sound made by coughing.

count /kount/ *v.* **1** To find out how
many: *Count* the petals on the
daisy. **2** To name numbers in
order: *Count* from 1 to 10. **3** To
be sure of: You can *count* on me.

coun·try /kun′trē/ *n., pl.* **countries**
1 A nation. **2** The land outside of
cities and towns: There are many
farms in the *country.*

coun·ty /koun′tē/ *n., pl.* **counties**
An area within a state: A *county*
has its own local officials.

cou·ple /kup′əl/ *n.* **1** Two or a few:
Rosa has a *couple* of things to do.
2 Two people who belong together.

course /kôrs/ *n.* A group of classes: a
cooking *course.*
—**of course** Certainly.

court /kôrt/ *n.* **1** Where trials are
held. **2** Where tennis or basket-
ball is played.

cous·in /kuz′(ə)n/ *n.* The son or
daughter of your uncle or aunt.

cov·er /kuv′ər/ *n.* Anything put over
something else: Nilda put a *cover*
on the frying pan.
—*v.* To be over or put something
over: Snow *covered* the ground.

co·zy /kō′zē/ *adj.* Warm and
comfortable: Matt felt *cozy* under
his blanket.

crash /krash/ *n.* **1** A loud noise.
2 One thing hitting something
else: a car *crash.*
—*v.* To hit with a loud noise: A
cup *crashed* on the floor.

crawl /krôl/ *v.* **1** To creep on hands
and knees. **2** To move slowly:
The cars *crawled* in heavy traffic.

cray·on /krā′on *or* krā′ən/ *n.* A
colored wax stick for drawing.

creek /krēk/ *n.* A small stream.

crook·ed /krŏŏk′id/ *adj.* **1** Not
straight. **2** Not honest: Their
plan sounds *crooked.*

---

act, āte, câre, ärt;   egg, ēven;   if, īce;   on, ōver, ôr;   bŏŏk, fŏŏd;   up, tûrn;
ə = a in *ago,* e in *listen,* i in *giraffe,* o in *pilot,* u in *circus;*   yŏŏ = u in *music;*   oil;   out;
chair; sing; shop; thank; that; zh in *treasure.*

crop /krop/ *n.* Something that is grown on a farm: Corn is a *crop*.

crown /kroun/ *n.* A wreath or band worn by a king or queen.
—*v.* To make a person king or queen.

crumb /krum/ *n.* **1** A tiny piece of bread or cake. **2** A tiny bit: There wasn't a *crumb* of food left.

cry /krī/ *v.* **cried, crying** **1** To weep or sob. **2** To call out; to shout: Sam *cried* for help.
—*n., pl.* **cries** A shout.

cup·board /kub′ərd/ *n.* A cabinet where dishes and food are kept.

D

dai·ly /dā′lē/ *adj., adv.* Once a day: My *daily* chore is feeding the cat. I eat breakfast *daily*.

dai·sy /dā′zē/ *n., pl.* **daisies** A white flower with a yellow center.

dance /dans/ *v.* **danced, dancing** To move in time to music.
—*n.* **1** A set of steps for dancing: The polka is a *dance*. **2** A party or gathering where people dance.

dan·ger /dān′jər/ *n.* Something that can hurt you: Fire is a *danger* to all of us.

dark /därk/ *adj.* **1** Without light: The sky is *dark* at night. **2** Almost black in color: Brown is a *dark* color.
—*n.* **1** Darkness: Don't be afraid of the *dark*. **2** Nightfall: Jenny was home before *dark*.

daugh·ter /dô′tər/ *n.* What a girl or woman is to her parents.

day·light /dā′līt′/ *n.* **1** The light of the sun. **2** Dawn; sunrise: I got up before *daylight*.

de·cide /di·sīd′/ *v.* **decided, deciding** To make up your mind: Adam *decided* to stay at home.

deep /dēp/ *adj.* **1** Very far from the top: a *deep* hole. **2** Dark in color: Navy is a *deep* blue.
—*adv.* In, at, or to a deep place: Miners work *deep* in the earth.

de·lay /di·lā′/ *v.* **1** To make late: Rain *delayed* the game. **2** To put off: The O'Neals *delayed* their trip.

de·light /di·līt′/ *n.* Great joy.
—*v.* To give joy: Children *delight* their parents.

de·ny /di·nī′/ *v.* **denied, denying** To say that something is not true: He *denied* that he had been there.

desk /desk/ *n.* A table with drawers used for writing or studying.

de·stroy /di·stroi′/ *v.* To break or ruin: Fire can *destroy* a forest.

de·tail /di·tāl′ *or* dē′tāl/ *n.* A small piece of information.

did·n't /did′(ə)nt/ Did not.

din·ner /din′ər/ *n.* The main meal of the day.

dish /dish/ *n., pl.* **dishes** **1** Something used to hold food. **2** A type of food: Spaghetti is my favorite *dish*.

di·vide /di·vīd′/ *v.* **divided, dividing** To make things or numbers into parts: Darin *divided* the clay into three pieces.

do /doo͞/ *v.* **did, done, doing** **1** To carry out a task: Alex *did* his homework. **2** To get along: Ginny *does* well at school. **3** To be right: This pencil will *do*. **4** *Do* is used to ask questions: *Do* you like green apples? **5** *Do* can take the place of a verb already used: Helga skates better than I *do*.

does·n't /duz′ənt/ Does not.

dol·lar /dol′ər/ *n.* A unit of money equal to 100 cents.

don't /dōnt/ Do not.

dot /dot/ *n.* A round mark: ·.
  —*v.* **dotted, dotting** To mark with a dot: Remember to *dot* your i's.

dou·ble /dub′əl/ *adj.* **1** Twice as much; twice as large: a *double* meat burger. **2** Having two parts: a *double* feature.
  —*v.* **doubled, doubling** To make twice as great: If you *double* 2, you get 4.

down·pour /doun′pôr′/ *n.* Heavy rain.

down·stairs /doun′stârz′/ *adv.* **1** Down the stairs. **2** On a lower floor: Tim is *downstairs.*

draw /drô/ *v.* **drew, drawn, drawing** To make a picture with a pencil or crayon.

draw·er /drôr/ *n.* A boxlike container that slides in and out.

dream /drēm/ *n.* **1** What goes through your mind when you are asleep. **2** Something you hope for: Al's *dream* is to be an actor.
  —*v.* To have a dream.

drill /dril/ *n.* **1** A tool used for making holes. **2** An exercise: We had a fire *drill* today.
  —*v.* **1** To make a hole with a drill. **2** To teach by giving a drill: Ms. Perkins *drilled* us in spelling.

drive /drīv/ *v.* **drove, driven, driving** **1** To run a car, bus, or truck. **2** To go or be carried in a car: Mr. Atkins *drove* me home.
  —*n.* A ride: Let's go for a *drive.*

drop /drop/ *v.* **dropped, dropping** **1** To fall or let fall: Don't *drop* crumbs on the rug. **2** To leave out: *Drop* the e in <u>race</u> before you add <u>ed</u>.
  —*n.* A tiny amount of liquid: I felt a *drop* of rain.

dry /drī/ *v.* **dried, drying** To remove water from: Joan *dried* the dishes.
  —*adj.* Not wet: Use the *dry* towel.

duck /duk/ *n.* A bird with a flat bill and webbed feet that swims.
  —*v.* To lower your head or move quickly: Sara *ducked* when I threw the ball.

dust /dust/ *n.* Tiny pieces of dirt.
  —*v.* To wipe away dust: Peggy *dusted* the table.

dwell /dwel/ *v.* To live or make your home: Animals *dwell* in the forest.

E

each /ēch/ *adj., pron.* Every one: *Each* boy sings well. I gave a sandwich to *each.*
  —*adv.* Apiece: Mom bought us two books *each.*

ea·gle /ē′gəl/ *n.* A hunting bird with sharp eyes and powerful wings.

---

act, āte, câre, ärt;   egg, ēven;   if, īce;   on, ōver, ôr;   bŏŏk, fōōd;   up, tûrn;
ə = a in *ago,* e in *listen,* i in *giraffe,* o in *pilot,* u in *circus;*   yōō = u in *music;*   oil;   out;
chair; sing; shop; thank; that; zh in *treasure.*

ear¹ /ir/ *n.* What people and animals use for hearing.

ear² /ir/ *n.* Where grain grows on some plants: an *ear* of corn.

ear·ly /ûr′lē/ *adv., adj.* **earlier, earliest** **1** Near the beginning: I get up *early* in the morning. **2** Before the regular time: Josh got home *early*.

earn /ûrn/ *v.* **1** To get money for doing work. **2** To get by trying hard: Ellen *earned* the prize.

earth /ûrth/ *n.* **1** The planet we live on. **2** Ground or soil: We planted seeds in the *earth*.

east /ēst/ *n., adj., adv.* A direction; where the sun comes up.

eas·y /ē′zē/ *adj.* **easier, easiest** **1** Not hard to do. **2** Without worry or trouble: an *easy* life.

edge /ej/ *n.* **1** Where something ends: the *edge* of the paper. **2** The cutting side of a knife.

egg /eg/ *n.* **1** An oval body with a hard shell laid by female birds. **2** The food that is inside an egg.

eight /āt/ *n., adj.* The word for *8*.

eighth /ātth *or* āth/ *adj.* Next after seventh.

eight·y /ā′tē/ *n., adj.* The word for *80*.

ei·ther /ē′t͟hər *or* ī′t͟hər/ *adj., pron., conj.* One or the other: *Either* puzzle is fun. You may do *either*. *Either* do it now or do it later. —*adv.* Also: Mindy doesn't want to go *either*.

e·lev·en /i·lev′ən/ *n., adj.* The word for *11*.

else /els/ *adj.* Other; besides: Do you want anything *else*?

emp·ty /emp′tē/ *adj.* Holding nothing: The box was *empty*.

—*v.* **emptied, emptying** To make empty: Ben *emptied* his pockets.

en·e·my /en′ə·mē/ *n., pl.* **enemies** A person who tries to harm another, or a country that fights another country in war.

en·joy /in·joi′/ *v.* To take pleasure in: Lou *enjoys* playing the piano.

e·nough /i·nuf′/ *adj.* Having the amount needed: There is *enough* turkey for two meals. —*n.* All that is needed: There is *enough* for everyone.

en·vy /en′vē/ *n.* The desire to have what someone else has: Nadia's coat made me green with *envy*. —*v.* **envied, envying** To feel envy toward: Pat *envied* his brother.

e·ven /ē′vən/ *adj.* **1** Flat and smooth: The floor is *even*. **2** Steady; regular: She drove at an *even* speed. **3** On the same level: The top of the bush was *even* with my chin. **4** Equal: The score was *even*. —*adv.* Still: an *even* better idea. —*v.* **1** To make or become level: The road *evens* out here. **2** To make equal: The touchdown *evened* the score.

eve·ning /ēv′ning/ *n.* The early part of nighttime.

ev·er /ev′ər/ *adv.* At any time: Did you *ever* go to the zoo?

eve·ry /ev′rē *or* ev′ər·ē/ *adj.* Each one: You got *every* answer right.

eve·ry·bod·y /ev′rē·bod′ē/ *pron.* Each person; everyone.

eve·ry·day /ev′rē·dā′/ *adj.* **1** Taking place each day: an *everyday* job. **2** Not special: *everyday* clothes.

eve·ry·one /ev′rē·wun′/ *pron.* Each person; everybody.

158

eve·ry·where /ev′rē·(h)wâr′/ *adv.* In all places; all around.

eye /ī/ *n.* What people and animals use for seeing.
—*v.* **eyed, eying** *or* **eyeing** To watch: The cat *eyed* the bird.

F

face /fās/ *n.*   **1** The front part of your head.   **2** A look: Miko made a funny *face.*
—*v.* **faced, facing**   **1** To turn toward: Everyone should *face* the teacher.   **2** To have the front toward: Our house *faces* the road.

fac·to·ry /fak′tər·ē/ *n., pl.* **factories** A place where things are made.

faint /fānt/ *v.* To become weak and pass out.
—*adj.*   **1** Dim; slight: There was a *faint* glow in the sky.   **2** Weak.

fair¹ /fâr/ *adj.*   **1** Following the rules; honest: It was a *fair* game.   **2** Not good and not bad: My test mark was *fair.*   **3** Clear; bright: The weather will be *fair* tomorrow.
—*adv.* In a fair way: Play *fair.*

fair² /fâr/ *n.*   **1** A showing of farm animals and farm goods.   **2** A sale of things: Our block had a *fair* to raise money.

fair·y /fâr′ē/ *n., pl.* **fairies** A tiny, make-believe being.

fall /fôl/ *v.* **fell, fallen, falling**   **1** To drop down: Laura *fell* off the horse.   **2** To pass into a state: George *fell* asleep.
—*n.*   **1** The season after summer.   **2** The act of falling: a bad *fall.*

fam·i·ly /fam′ə·lē *or* fam′lē/ *n., pl.* **families**   **1** Parents and their children.   **2** Animals or plants that are related in some way: Lions are part of the cat *family.*

far /fär/ *adv., adj.* At a long way away: Our school is *far* from here.

farm /färm/ *n.* Land where crops are grown and animals are raised.
—*v.* To have and run a farm.

fa·ther /fä′thər/ *n.* A male parent.

fawn /fôn/ *n.* A baby deer.

feast /fēst/ *n.* A large, special meal.
—*v.* To eat a feast.

fed /fed/ *v.* Past tense and past participle of *feed.*

feed /fēd/ *v.* **fed, feeding** To give food to: Jerry *fed* the birds.

feel /fēl/ *v.* **felt, feeling**   **1** To touch.   **2** To be aware of: I *feel* the wind blowing.   **3** To be: Hal *feels* sad.

fell /fel/ *v.* Past tense of *fall.*

felt /felt/ *v.* Past tense and past participle of *feel.*

fence /fens/ *n.* A wall of wood or wire put around a piece of land.

fif·teen /fif′tēn′/ *n., adj.* The word for *15.*

fifth /fifth/ *adj.* Next after fourth.

fif·ty /fif′tē/ *n., adj.* The word for *50.*

---

act, āte, câre, ärt;   egg, ēven;   if, īce;   on, ōver, ôr;   bŏok, fōod;   up, tûrn;
ə = **a** in *ago,* **e** in *listen,* **i** in *giraffe,* **o** in *pilot,* **u** in *circus;*   yōō = **u** in *music;*   **oil**;   **out**;
chair; sing; shop; thank; that; zh in *treasure.*

fight /fīt/ *n.*   **1** A battle.   **2** A bad quarrel.

—*v.* **fought, fighting**   **1** To make war.   **2** To quarrel.   **3** To struggle against: Doctors *fight* disease.

fi·nal /fī′nəl/ *adj.*   **1** Last: Today is the *final* day of school.   **2** Not to be changed: My choice is *final*.

find /fīnd/ *v.* **found, finding**   **1** To come upon: I *found* a watch at the beach.   **2** To get back something lost: Mark *found* his glasses.   **3** To learn: Allison *found* the answer to the math problem.

fin·ger /fing′gər/ *n.* One of the five parts that make up the end of your hand.

first /fûrst/ *adj., adv.* Before everything else: Sally was *first* in line.

flag /flag/ *n.* A piece of cloth with special colors and designs on it.

flash /flash/ *n., pl.* **flashes**   **1** A sudden bright light.   **2** A short time: Russ finished in a *flash*.

—*v.*   **1** To give a quick bright light: Lightning *flashed* in the sky.   **2** To move quickly: Diane *flashed* by on her bike.

flat /flat/ *adj.* **flatter, flattest**   **1** Smooth and level.   **2** Without air: a *flat* tire.

—*adv.* In a flat way: Lie *flat* on your back.

flew /floo/ *v.* Past tense and past participle of *fly*[1].

float /flōt/ *v.* To rest on water or in the air: Eva can *float* on her back. The balloon *floated* away.

—*n.* A display in a parade.

flock /flok/ *n.*   **1** A group of birds or animals.   **2** A large crowd: *Flocks* of people came to the park.

floor /flôr/ *n.*   **1** The part of a room you stand on.   **2** A story of a building: We live on the third *floor*.

flour /flour/ *n.* A fine powder made from wheat or other grain.

fly[1] /flī/ *v.* **flew, flown, flying**   **1** To go through the air: Birds can *fly*.   **2** To wave in the air: The flags are *flying*.   **3** To cause to float in the air: Betsy is *flying* her kite.   **4** To go by plane.

—*n., pl.* **flies** In baseball, a ball hit high in the air.

fly[2] /flī/ *n., pl.* **flies** An insect with two wings that flies.

fog·gy /fog′ē/ *adj.* **foggier, foggiest** Full of fog or mist: It was so *foggy* that we could not see.

fold /fōld/ *v.* To bend one part over another: *Fold* the paper in half.

fol·low /fol′ō/ *v.*   **1** To go along behind: The dog *followed* me home.   **2** To come after: Fall *follows* summer.   **3** To obey: Max *follows* orders well.

foot·ball /foot′bôl′/ *n.*   **1** An oval ball.   **2** A team game played with such a ball.

for·ev·er /fôr·ev′ər/ *adv.* Always: I'll be your friend *forever*.

for·get /fər·get′/ *v.* **forgot, forgotten, forgetting**   **1** To fail to remember or think of.   **2** To leave behind: Ken *forgot* his book.

for·got /fər·got′/ v. Past tense and past participle of *forget*.

for·ty /fôr′tē/ n., adj. The word for *40*.

fos·sil /fos′əl/ n. The mark of a very old plant or animal in a rock.

fought /fôt/ v. Past tense and past participle of *fight*.

found /found/ v. Past tense and past participle of *find*.

four /fôr/ n., adj. The word for *4*.

fourth /fôrth/ adj. Next after third.

frame /frām/ n. A border around something: a picture *frame*.
—v. **framed, framing** To put something in a frame.

free /frē/ adj. **1** Not costing money. **2** Having liberty: You are *free* to leave when you want to.
—v. **freed, freeing** To let out of: They *freed* the fox from a trap.
—adv. Without paying: Parents may come *free* to the school play.

free·dom /frē′dəm/ n. Being free; liberty: Americans value *freedom*.

fresh /fresh/ adj. **1** Newly made or gotten: *fresh* fruit. **2** Clean and cool: *fresh* air.

Fri. Abbreviation for *Friday*.

Fri·day /frī′dē/ n. The sixth day of the week.

from /frum, from, *or* frəm/ prep. **1** Starting at: We drove *from* Ohio to Iowa. **2** Sent or given by: I got a letter *from* my aunt.

frown /froun/ v. To look angry or sad.
—n. A sad or angry look.

fudge /fuj/ n. Soft chocolate candy.

fun·ny /fun′ē/ adj. **funnier, funniest** Able to make you laugh.

fur /fûr/ n. The hair on the skin of many animals.
—adj. Made of fur: a *fur* coat.

G

gar·den /gär′dən/ n. A place where flowers or vegetables are grown.

gate /gāt/ n. The doorlike part of a fence or wall.

gath·er /gath′ər/ v. **1** To bring together: Simon *gathered* up the test papers. **2** To come together: The family *gathered* for dinner.

geese /gēs/ n. Plural of *goose*.

gen·tle /jen′təl/ adj. Kind and tender: Be *gentle* with the baby.

ghost /gōst/ n. A spirit that seems to appear to living people.

gi·ant /jī′ənt/ n. A very large, strong person in fairy tales.
—adj. Very large; huge: We saw a *giant* elephant at the circus.

gin·ger·bread /jin′jər·bred′/ n. A cake flavored with ginger.

gi·raffe /jə·raf′/ n. An animal with a very long neck and spotted skin.

girl /gûrl/ n. A female child.

give /giv/ v. **gave, given, giving** To hand over; to offer: *Give* me your hand.

---

act, āte, câre, ärt; egg, ēven; if, īce; on, ōver, ôr; book, food; up, tûrn;
ə = a in *ago*, e in *listen*, i in *giraffe*, o in *pilot*, u in *circus*; yoo = u in *music*; oil; out;
chair; sing; shop; thank; that; zh in *treasure*.

glad /glad/ *adj.* Pleased or happy: I'll be *glad* to come.

glass /glas/ *n., pl.* **glasses** **1** A clear material that breaks easily. **2** A drinking cup. **3** (*pl.*) Two pieces of glass or plastic used to help people see better.

good·ness /good′nis/ *n.* The condition of being good: Caring for others is a sign of *goodness*.

goose /goos/ *n., pl.* **geese** A bird with a long neck that looks like a duck.

grab /grab/ *v.* **grabbed, grabbing** To take hold of suddenly: Chad *grabbed* my arm to stop me.

grade /grād/ *n.* **1** The school year or level: Mei is in the third *grade*. **2** A mark given in school: Rae gets good *grades* in school.

grand /grand/ *adj.* **1** Large, important: The mayor lives in a *grand* house. **2** Complete: What is the *grand* total? **3** Very good: We had a *grand* time at the zoo.

grand·fa·ther /gran(d)′fä′thər/ *n.* Your father's or mother's father.

grand·moth·er /gran(d)′muth′ər/ *n.* Your father's or mother's mother.

grape /grāp/ *n.* A fruit that grows in bunches on vines.

grass /gras/ *n.* A plant with green blades that covers the ground.

grew /groo/ *v.* Past tense of *grow*.

groan /grōn/ *n.* A sound of pain.
—*v.* To make such a sound: Callie *groaned* because her arm hurt.

ground /ground/ *n.* Earth's surface; soil: The *ground* was wet.

group /groop/ *n.* Several people or things together.
—*v.* To make a group: Darrel *grouped* his marbles by color.

grow /grō/ *v.* **grew, grown, growing** **1** To become larger or taller: Puppies *grow* very quickly. **2** To plant something: We *grow* tomatoes.

grown /grōn/ *v.* Past participle of *grow*.

guess /ges/ *n., pl.* **guesses** An idea you have without knowing for sure: I think it will rain, but that's just a *guess*.
—*v.* **1** To make a guess. **2** To suppose: I *guess* you are right.

gup·py /gup′ē/ *n., pl.* **guppies** A tiny colorful fish.

gym /jim/ *n.* Short for *gymnasium*. A large room where people play games and exercise.

H

hair /hâr/ *n.* The threadlike strands that grow on your head.

hair·cut /hâr′kut′/ *n.* The cutting of hair or the way hair is cut.

half /haf/ *n., pl.* **halves** One of two equal parts.
—*adj.* Being half: a *half* hour.
—*adv.* Partly: Don is *half* asleep.

hand /hand/ *n.* **1** The end part of your arm. **2** One of the pointers on a clock or watch.
—*v.* To give or pass: Ken *handed* the money to the clerk.

hap·pen /hap′ən/ *v.* To take place: Nothing *happened* after you left.

hap·py /hap′ē/ *adj.* **happier, happiest** Full of joy; glad.

hard /härd/ *adj.* **1** Solid: *hard* as a rock. **2** Not easy: a *hard* test.
—*adv.* With effort or force: Penny works *hard*.

have·n't /hav′ənt/ Have not.

hay /hā/ *n.* Grass that is cut and dried to feed animals.

head·ache /hed'āk'/ *n.* A pain in your head.

hear /hir/ *v.* **heard, hearing** To take in sounds through your ears.

heard /hûrd/ *v.* Past tense and past participle of *hear.*

heart /härt/ *n.* **1** The organ in your body that pumps blood. **2** Something that has this shape: ♡.

hel·lo /hə·lō'/ *interj.* A greeting.

help /help/ *v.* To be useful; to do what is needed: Ethel *helps* around the house.
—*n.* A person or thing that helps: Lena is a great *help* to Grandma.

here /hir/ *adv.* In or to this place: Let's sit *here.* Bring it *here.*

her·self /hər·self'/ *pron.* Her own self: She sang to *herself.*

he's /hēz/ **1** He is. **2** He has.

hid /hid/ *v.* Past tense of *hide*[1].

hide[1] /hīd/ *v.* **hid, hidden, hiding** **1** To put out of sight: Gene *hid* the gift in the closet. **2** To hide oneself: Keisha *hid* behind a bush.

hide[2] /hīd/ *n.* The skin of an animal.

high /hī/ *adj.* **1** Far up. **2** Great in cost: The price is too *high.*
—*adv.* To a high place: The building reaches *high* in the sky.

high·way /hī'wā'/ *n.* A main road.

hike /hīk/ *n.* A long walk: We went for a *hike* in the woods.
—*v.* **hiked, hiking** To take a hike.

him·self /him·self'/ *pron.* His own self: He taught *himself* to skate.

hob·by /hob'ē/ *n., pl.* **hobbies** A special interest: Steve's *hobby* is collecting stamps.

hold /hōld/ *v.* **held, holding** **1** To take and keep: Please *hold* my coat. **2** To keep in place: Glue will *hold* it together. **3** To keep back: *Hold* your breath. **4** To have: We *held* a meeting.

hole /hōl/ *n.* An open space in or through something solid.

hol·low /hol'ō/ *adj.* Empty inside: Squirrels live in that *hollow* tree.

hop /hop/ *v.* **hopped, hopping** **1** To move the way a rabbit does. **2** To jump on one foot. **3** To jump over or into: Ted *hopped* into bed.

hope /hōp/ *v.* **hoped, hoping** To wish or expect: I *hope* to do well.
—*n.* **1** Trust that what you wish for will happen. **2** Something hoped for. **3** Cause for hope: Roxie is our team's only *hope.*

horn /hôrn/ *n.* **1** A hard bony growth on an animal's head: Cows have *horns.* **2** Something that makes a warning sound: a car *horn.* **3** A musical instrument.

horse /hôrs/ *n.* A four-legged animal with hoofs and a mane.

house /hous/ *n., pl.* **houses** /hou'zəz/ A building in which people live.

---

act, āte, câre, ärt; egg, ēven; if, īce; on, ōver, ôr; bŏŏk, fōōd; up, tûrn;
ə = a in *ago*, e in *listen*, i in *giraffe*, o in *pilot*, u in *circus*; yōō = u in *music*; oil; out;
chair; sing; shop; thank; that; zh in *treasure.*

163

how /hou/ *adv.* **1** In what way: *How* did you do it? **2** To what degree: *How* tall is Aaron?

hun·dred /hun'drid/ *n., adj.* The word for *100*.

hun·gry /hung'grē/ *adj.* Wanting or needing food.

hunt /hunt/ *v.* **1** To kill animals for food. **2** To look for: I *hunted* all over for my lost scarf.
—*n.* A search: a treasure *hunt*.

hur·ry /hûr'ē/ *v.* **hurried, hurrying**
1 To move or act quickly: Pam *hurried* to get home on time. **2** To make someone else move or act quickly: Don't *hurry* me.
—*n.* Eagerness to do something quickly: Grace was in a *hurry*.

hurt /hûrt/ *v.* To feel or cause pain or harm: Troy *hurt* himself.

I

ice /īs/ *n.* Frozen water.
—*v.* **iced, icing** To put frosting on a cake.

ill /il/ *adj.* Feeling sick.

I'll /īl/ **1** I will. **2** I shall.

I'm /īm/ I am.

inch /inch/ *n., pl.* **inches** A unit of length.

in·sect /in'sekt/ *n.* A very small animal with six legs and often wings: Bees and flies are *insects*.

in·side /in'sīd' *or* in'sīd'/ *adv.* Indoors.
—*prep.* In or within: Dan put his socks *inside* his shoes.
—*n.* The part that is inside: The *inside* of the house is white.

in·to /in'tōō/ *prep.* **1** To the inside: Walk *into* the room. **2** To the form of: The ice turned *into* water.

in·vite /in·vīt'/ *v.* **invited, inviting**
To ask someone to come: Joanne *invited* me to her party.

is /iz/ *v.* Form of the verb *to be*. You use *is* after names, words for one thing, and *he, she,* or *it*.

is·n't /iz'ənt/ Is not.

it's /its/ **1** It is. **2** It has.

J

jack·et /jak'it/ *n.* A short coat.

jam¹ /jam/ **jammed, jamming** *v.* To squeeze into a small space: He *jammed* his books into his bag.

jam² /jam/ *n.* Fruit cooked with sugar until thick: strawberry *jam*.

jar /jär/ *n.* A bottle with a wide top.

jaw /jô/ *n.* The upper or lower bone of a mouth: A whale has huge *jaws*.

jet /jet/ *n.* A kind of airplane.

job /job/ *n.* Work that is done, often for money.

join /join/ *v.* **1** To bring or come together: We all *joined* hands. **2** To become a member of a group.

joke /jōk/ *n.* Something that makes you laugh; a funny story.
—*v.* **joked, joking** To do or say something funny.

joy /joi/ *n.* Great happiness.

judge /juj/ *n.* **1** The person who makes decisions in a court of law. **2** The person who decides who wins a race or contest.
—*v.* **judged, judging** **1** To act as a judge in court. **2** To decide who wins: Liza *judged* the contest.

jug /jug/ *n.* A large bottle with a narrow neck and a handle.

juice /jōōs/ *n.* The liquid part of fruits, vegetables, or meat.

jump /jump/ *v.* **1** To leap up or over: The cat *jumped* on the window sill. **2** To jerk suddenly: Ken *jumped* when the phone rang. —*n.* A leap.

jun·gle /jung′gəl/ *n.* A thick forest where wild animals live.

just /just/ *adv.* **1** A little while ago: We *just* got here. **2** Barely: Alfredo got here *just* in time. **3** Only: I'm *just* tired. **4** Very: This meal is *just* delicious.

K

keep /kēp/ *v.* **kept, keeping 1** To have and not give up: You may *keep* that pencil. **2** To hold back: *Keep* the dog off the sofa. **3** To continue: Let's *keep* trying.

kept /kept/ *v.* Past tense and past participle of *keep*.

ket·tle /ket′(ə)l/ *n.* **1** A large pot. **2** A pot with a spout; teakettle.

key /kē/ *n.* **1** A small metal thing used to open or close a lock. **2** Something that explains or gives answers: an answer *key* for a test. **3** One of the parts pressed on a piano or typewriter.

kick /kik/ *v.* To hit with your foot. —*n.* A blow with the foot: Lee gave the stone a hard *kick*.

kind·ness /kīnd′nis/ *n.* Being kind and nice: Nicky treats everyone with *kindness*.

kiss /kis/ *v.* To touch someone with your lips as a sign of love. —*n.* The act of kissing: Jake gave Grandma a hug and a *kiss*.

kitch·en /kich′ən/ *n.* The room where food is prepared.

kit·ten /kit′(ə)n/ *n.* A young cat.

knead /nēd/ *v.* To mix dough using your hands to push and squeeze.

knee /nē/ *n.* The joint in the middle of your leg and the area around it.

kneel /nēl/ *v.* **knelt** *or* **kneeled, kneeling** To go down on your knees.

knew /n(y)o͞o/ *v.* Past tense of *know*.

knife /nīf/ *n.* **knives** A tool with a sharp side for cutting.

knit /nit/ *v.* **knit** *or* **knitted, knitting** To make clothes using yarn and long needles.

knock /nok/ *v.* **1** To hit. **2** To make a pounding noise: *Knock* on the door. —*n.* A pounding noise: We heard a *knock* at the door.

knot /not/ *n.* A fastening made by tying ropes or string. —*v.* **knotted, knotting** To tie in a knot.

know /nō/ *v.* **knew, known, knowing 1** To be sure: I *know* you are wrong. **2** To understand: Ira *knows* how to do it. **3** To be friends with: We *know* the Wilsons.

known /nōn/ *v.* Past participle of *know*.

---

act, āte, câre, ärt;   egg, ēven;   if, īce;   on, ōver, ôr;   bŏŏk, fo͞od;   up, tûrn;
ə = **a** in *ago*, **e** in *listen*, **i** in *giraffe*, **o** in *pilot*, **u** in *circus*;   y**o͞o** = **u** in *music*;   oil;   out;
chair; si**ng**; **sh**op; **th**ank; **th**at; **zh** in *treasure*.

L

la·dy /lā′dē/ *n.*, *pl.* **ladies** **1** A woman. **2** A woman with good manners.

lake /lāk/ *n.* A body of water.

lamb /lam/ *n.* A young sheep.

land /land/ *n.* **1** The part of Earth that is not covered by water. **2** A country.
—*v.* To arrive on land: The spaceship *landed* on the moon.

large /lärj/ *adj.* **larger, largest** Big in size or amount.

last¹ /last/ *adj.* **1** Coming at the end: I ate the *last* piece. **2** Just before: We saw the Itos *last* month.
—*adv.* **1** Coming at the end: Bob woke up *last*. **2** Most recent: When were you *last* at the zoo?

last² /last/ *v.* To go on: The picnic *lasted* all day.

late /lāt/ *adj.*, *adv.* After or past a certain time: He came *late*.

lay¹ /lā/ *v.* **laid, laying** To put down: *Lay* your coats on the bed.

lay² /lā/ *v.* Past tense of *lie¹*.

learn /lûrn/ *v.* **1** To get skill in or knowledge: Diego *learned* to play baseball. **2** To find out: Janice *learned* why Nina left early.

leave /lēv/ *v.* **left, leaving** **1** To go away. **2** To let stay behind: Tad *left* his books at school. **3** To let someone else do something: Just *leave* everything to me.

ledge /lej/ *n.* A narrow shelf: Put the plant on the window *ledge*.

left¹ /left/ *n.* The opposite of right.
—*adj.*, *adv.* On or to the left: Give me your *left* hand. Turn *left*.

left² /left/ *v.* Past tense and past participle of *leave*.

leg /leg/ *n.* **1** One of the parts of the body used to stand and walk. **2** Something like a leg: a table *leg*.

less /les/ *adj.* Smaller in number or amount: Teddy has *less* money.
—*n.* An amount: I did *less* than I planned to do.
—*adv.* In a smaller amount: This book costs *less* than that one.

les·son /les′(ə)n/ *n.* Something to be learned or taught: Peter did the math *lesson*.

let /let/ *v.* To allow: Will your parents *let* you go to the zoo?

let's /lets/ Let us: *Let's* go now.

let·ter /let′ər/ *n.* **1** One of the parts of the alphabet. **2** A written message: I mailed a *letter*.

lev·el /lev′əl/ *adj.* Smooth or even: The ground is *level* over there.

li·brar·y /lī′brer′ē or lī′brə·rē/ *n.*, *pl.* **libraries** A place where books are kept.

lie¹ /lī/ *v.* **lay, lain, lying** To rest in a flat position: Sandy is *lying* on the couch.

lie² /lī/ *n.* Something told that is not true: Jessie told me a *lie*.
—*v.* **lied, lying** To tell a lie.

life /līf/ *n.*, *pl.* **lives** **1** The state of being alive: There are no signs of *life* on Mars. **2** The period of being alive: I have lived here all my *life*. **3** A way of living: Firefighters have a dangerous *life*.

lift /lift/ *v.* To pick up and raise: Conchita *lifted* her little sister.
—*n.* A ride: We got a *lift* home.

light¹ /līt/ *n.* **1** Brightness: We cannot see without *light*. **2** Something that gives light.
—*v.* **lit or lighted, lighting** **1** To give light: The lantern *lighted* our

path.   **2** To set fire to: Mom will *light* the candles.

—*adj.* Pale in color: a *light* color.

light² /līt/ *adj.* Not heavy: as *light* as a feather.

limb /lim/ *n.* A branch of a tree.

line /līn/ *n.*   **1** A straight mark.   **2** A row: There was a long *line* of people at the checkout counter.

li·on /lī′ən/ *n.* A large, powerful animal of the cat family.

list /list/ *n.* A group of things written down in order: Mom takes a shopping *list* to the market.

—*v.* To make a list.

lis·ten /lis′(ə)n/ *v.* To pay attention; to try to hear: *Listen* carefully.

live¹ /liv/ *v.* **lived, living**   **1** To be alive: Grandpa *lived* for eighty years.   **2** To make your home: They *live* in Iowa.

live² /līv/ *adj.* Being alive.

load /lōd/ *n.* Something carried: A mule can carry a heavy *load*.

—*v.* To fill or put on: Lisa *loaded* her camera. The movers *loaded* the furniture on the truck.

look·out /look′out′/ *n.*   **1** The act of watching out: Be on the *lookout* for a ship with a yellow flag.   **2** A person who watches.

lose /looz/ *v.* **lost, losing**   **1** To be unable to find: Lori *lost* her scarf.   **2** To fail to keep: Don't *lose* your temper.   **3** To fail to win.

loud /loud/ *adj.* Not quiet; noisy.

love /luv/ *n.* A strong feeling.

—*v.* **loved, loving**   **1** To have a deep feeling for: Parents *love* their children.   **2** To like very much: Cindy *loves* to swim.

low /lō/ *adj.*   **1** Not high: The truck cannot go under the *low* bridge.   **2** Not loud: a *low* voice.

loy·al /loi′əl/ *adj.* Faithful: Our dog is very *loyal*.

luck·y /luk′ē/ *adj.* **luckier, luckiest** Having or bringing good luck: You were *lucky* to win.

lunch /lunch/ *n.* The meal eaten in the middle of the day.

M

ma·chine /mə·shēn′/ *n.* Something that does work: a sewing *machine*.

mag·ic /maj′ik/ *n.* The art of pretending to do things that are not possible.

—*adj.* Able to work magic: I will wave my *magic* wand.

mail /māl/ *n.* Letters and packages handled by the post office.

—*v.* To send a letter or package.

main /mān/ *adj.* Most important: Oak Avenue is the *main* street.

man·age /man′ij/ *v.* **managed, managing**   **1** To get by: How did you *manage* to do that alone?   **2** To be in charge: Ms. Ramos *manages* a store.

---

act, āte, câre, ärt;   egg, ēven;   if, īce;   on, ōver, ôr;   book, food;   up, tûrn;
ə = a in *ago*, e in *listen*, i in *giraffe*, o in *pilot*, u in *circus*;   yoo = u in *music*;   oil;   out;
chair;   sing;   shop;   thank;   that;   zh in *treasure*.

mane /mān/ *n.* The long hair on a horse's neck or around a male lion's face.

mar·ble /mär′bəl/ *n.* **1** A small glass ball used for games. **2** A hard stone used for buildings and statues: The floors are of *marble*.

mar·ket /mär′kit/ *n.* **1** A place where things are bought and sold: The farmer brought his fruit to *market*. **2** A store that sells food.

mar·ry /mar′ē/ *v.* **married, marrying** **1** To become husband and wife. **2** To join as husband and wife: The judge *married* my aunt and uncle.

mat·ter /mat′ər/ *n.* Something that troubles you: What is the *matter*? —*v.* To be of importance: Doing well in school *matters* to me.

may /mā/ *v.* **1** To have permission to: You *may* leave the room. **2** To be possible: It *may* rain today.

may·be /mā′bē/ *adv.* Perhaps; possibly: *Maybe* we'll go tomorrow.

meal /mēl/ *n.* Food eaten at one time: I eat three *meals* a day.

mean[1] /mēn/ *v.* **meant, meaning** **1** To want to: I didn't *mean* to trip you. **2** To have as its sense: What does this word *mean*?

mean[2] /mēn/ *adj.* Cruel.

mean·while /mēn′(h)wīl′/ *adv.* At the same time.

mea·sles /mē′zəlz/ *n.* A disease that makes your skin break out in red, itchy spots.

meat /mēt/ *n.* The flesh of animals used as food.

meet /mēt/ *v.* **met, meeting** **1** To come together: Let's *meet* at the corner. **2** To get to know: I *met* Charlie only a year ago.

melt /melt/ *v.* To get soft or become liquid: Butter *melts* on hot toast.

mem·o·ry /mem′ər·ē/ *n., pl.* **memories** **1** The ability to remember: Eliza has a very good *memory* for names. **2** What is remembered: I have happy *memories* of my vacation.

mess /mes/ *n.* A dirty or not neat condition: Your room is a *mess*. —*v.* To make untidy: Don't *mess* up the living room.

mid·dle /mid′(ə)l/ *n.* The center or halfway point.

mid·night /mid′nīt′/ *n.* Twelve o'clock at night.

milk /milk/ *n.* A white liquid from cows or other female animals. —*v.* To get milk from: Davey helped the farmer *milk* the cows.

mis·take /mis·tāk′/ *n.* Something that is done wrong.

Mon. Abbreviation for *Monday*.

Mon·day /mun′dē *or* mun′dā/ *n.* The second day of the week.

more /môr/ *adj.* **1** Greater in number or amount: Rex has *more* pencils than I have. **2** Additional: I bought *more* pencils today. —*n.* An amount: *More* of my pencils are new. —*adv.* **1** In a greater amount: I write *more* now. **2** Again: Tell me once *more*.

morn·ing /môr′ning/ *n.* The time of day from sunrise until noon.

mo·tel /mō·tel′/ *n.* A place where travelers can stay overnight.

mo·tor /mō′tər/ *n.* The engine that makes cars and other machines go. —*adj.* Run by a motor: a *motor* boat.

mouse /mous/ *n., pl.* **mice** A small animal with a pointed nose and a long tail: Our cat catches *mice*.

mouth /mouth/ *n.* **1** The opening in your face used for speaking and eating. **2** An opening like a mouth: the *mouth* of a jar.

move /mōōv/ *v.* **moved, moving 1** To go from one place to another: The car *moved* down the street. **2** To change where you live: The Engels *moved* to Grant Street. **3** To change position: The sleeping child didn't *move*.

my·self /mī·self′/ *pron.* My own self: I saw *myself* in the mirror.

N

nail /nāl/ *n.* **1** A thin pointed piece of metal used to hold wood together. **2** The thin hornlike layer at the end of a finger or toe: Stop biting your *nails*. —*v.* To put something together with nails.

name /nām/ *n.* What someone or something is called. —*v.* **named, naming 1** To give a name: They *named* the baby Inga. **2** To tell the name of: Can you *name* all fifty states?

nap /nap/ *n.* A short sleep. —*v.* **napped, napping** To sleep for a short time: The baby *naps* every afternoon.

nar·row /nar′ō/ *adj.* Not wide: The road was too *narrow* for two cars.

neat /nēt/ *adj.* **1** Clean and tidy. **2** Clever: That's a *neat* trick.

neck /nek/ *n.* The part of your body between your head and shoulders.

new /n(y)ōō/ *adj.* **1** Not old. **2** Started a short time ago: The *new* school year started last week.

news·pa·per /n(y)ōōz′pā′pər/ *n.* Sheets of paper with news stories on them: We read about the parade in the *newspaper*.

nice /nīs/ *adj.* **nicer, nicest** Pleasant; kind.

nick·el /nik′əl/ *n.* A coin worth five cents.

night /nīt/ *n.* The time between sunset and sunrise.

nine /nīn/ *n., adj.* The word for *9*.

nine·teen /nīn′tēn′/ *n., adj.* The word for *19*.

ninth /nīnth/ *n., adj.* Next after eighth.

noise /noiz/ *n.* Sound, especially loud sound: The crowd made a lot of *noise*.

noon /nōōn/ *n.* Twelve o'clock in the daytime.

north /nôrth/ *n., adj., adv.* A direction; the opposite of south.

not /not/ *adv.* In no way: I did *not* go.

no·tice /nō′tis/ *v.* **noticed, noticing** To see; to pay attention to: Do you *notice* anything different?

---

act, āte, câre, ärt;   egg, ēven;   if, īce;   on, ōver, ôr;   bŏŏk, fōōd;   up, tûrn;
ə = **a** in *ago*, **e** in *listen*, **i** in *giraffe*, **o** in *pilot*, **u** in *circus;*   yōō = **u** in *music;*   oil;   out;
chair; sing; shop; thank; that; zh in *treasure.*

now /nou/ *adv.* **1** At this time. **2** Because of what has happened: *Now* I'll never know the answer.

num·ber /num′bər/ *n.* **1** A unit in math. **2** An amount: I have a *number* of things to do.
—*v.* To give numbers to: Fay *numbered* the pages of her book.

o

oak /ōk/ *n.* **1** A tree that bears acorns. **2** The wood of this tree.
—*adj.* Made of oak.

o·bey /ō·bā′/ *v.* To do as you are told: My dog *obeys* me.

odd /od/ *adj.* **1** Strange, unusual: That is an *odd* house. **2** Not able to be divided by 2: *odd* numbers.

off /ôf *or* of/ *prep.* Away from: The pillow fell *off* the bed.
—*adv.* Not on: Take *off* your coat.

oil /oil/ *n.* A greasy liquid.
—*v.* To put oil on: We *oiled* the gate so it would not squeak.

old /ōld/ *adj.* **1** Having lived for a long time: Grandpa is an *old* man. **2** Of age: Thomas is eight years *old.* **3** Not new: James wore *old* jeans. **4** Known for a long time: Keith and Otis are *old* friends.

once /wuns/ *adv.* **1** One time: We go on a trip *once* a year. **2** At one time (in the past): I *once* saw a purple and red car.

on·ly /ōn′lē/ *adv.* Just: You have *only* one hour to play.
—*adj.* Alone: He is the *only* boy on the team.

oth·er /uth′ər/ *adj.* **1** Different: Do you want this crayon or the *other* one? **2** More: Do you want *other* books to read besides this one?
—*pron.* A different person or thing: Ricardo likes to help *others.*

our /our/ *pron.* Belonging to us: *Our* house is yellow.

our·selves /our·selvz′/ *pron.* Us and no one else: We made it *ourselves.*

out·side /out′sīd′ *or* out′sīd′/ *adv.* Outdoors: We played *outside.*
—*n.* The part that is out: We painted the *outside* of the house.
—*prep.* Out of: Put your boots *outside* the door.
—*adj.* On the outside: The *outside* shell of a nut is hard.

o·ver /ō′vər/ *prep.* On top of.
—*adv.* **1** Above. **2** Again: You must write your paper *over* because it is messy. **3** To a certain place: Bring it *over* here.
—*adj.* Finished: School is *over* at three o'clock.

owl /oul/ *n.* A night bird with large eyes and a hooked beak.

own /ōn/ *v.* To have in your possession: I *own* a bicycle.
—*adj.* Belonging to: my *own* room.

p

pack /pak/ *n.* A large bundle to be carried by a person or animal.
—*v.* **1** To put things in a package, box, or suitcase. **2** To crowd or fill up: People *packed* into the bus.

pack·age /pak′ij/ *n.* **1** Something wrapped up or tied up: We mailed a *package* to my brother at camp. **2** The box that holds something: The directions are on the *package.*

pad·dle /pad′(ə)l/ *n.* A short oar.
—*v.* **paddled, paddling** **1** To use a paddle to move a boat. **2** To move your hands and feet in water: The children *paddled* about in the lake.

page /pāj/ *n.* One of the sheets of paper in a book or magazine.

paid /pād/ *v.* Past tense and past participle of *pay.*

pain /pān/ *n.* Ache; soreness.

paint /pānt/ *n.* Colored liquid that is spread on something to make it that color.
—*v.* **1** To spread paint on. **2** To make a picture with paint.

pair /pâr/ *n.* Two people or things that go together: a *pair* of shoes.

pan·cake /pan′kāk′/ *n.* A thin flat cake fried in a pan.

pane /pān/ *n.* A sheet of glass put in the frame of a window: This window has a broken *pane.*

pa·per /pā′pər/ *n.* **1** Material used for writing, printing, and wrapping things. **2** A piece of paper with writing on it: Barney handed in his *paper.* **3** A newspaper.
—*adj.* Made of paper: Joy made a *paper* airplane.

pa·rade /pə·rād′/ *n.* A march of people with bands and floats.
—*v.* **parade, parading** To show off: He *paraded* around in his costume.

par·ent /pâr′ənt/ *n.* A person's mother or father.

park /pärk/ *n.* Land with trees, grass, and playgrounds.
—*v.* To put a car somewhere and leave it: *Park* the car over there.

part /pärt/ *n.* **1** A piece of a whole. **2** Share: We all must do our *part.* **3** A role in a play. **4** Where hair is divided after combing: The *part* in Lynn's hair is crooked.
—*v.* **1** To divide into pieces. **2** To make a part in your hair.

par·ty /pär′tē/ *n., pl.* **parties** **1** A group of people gathered together to have fun. **2** A group of people who work to elect government leaders: the Democratic *party.*

paste /pāst/ *n.* A thick white mixture used to stick things together.
—*v.* **pasted, pasting** To fasten with paste.

pat /pat/ *n.* A light touch.
—*v.* **patted, patting** To touch lightly: *Pat* the dog's head.

patch /pach/ *n., pl.* **patches** A piece of cloth used to cover a hole or weak spot: Mom put *patches* on the knees of my jeans.
—*v.* **1** To put back together: Dad *patched* together the broken bowl. **2** To put a patch on.

path /path/ *n.* A walk or trail.

pause /pôz/ *n.* A short stop.
—*v.* **paused, pausing** To make a pause: The speaker *paused* to drink some water.

paw /pô/ *n.* An animal's foot with nails or claws.

---

act, āte, cåre, ärt;   egg, ēven;   if, īce;   on, ōver, ôr;   bo͞ok, fo͞od;   up, tûrn;
ə = a in *ago*, e in *listen*, i in *giraffe*, o in *pilot*, u in *circus*;   yo͞o = u in *music*;   oil;   out;
chair;   sing;   shop;   thank;   that;   zh in *treasure.*

pay /pā/ *v.* **paid, paying** To give money for something: Dad *paid* for my bike.

—*n.* Money you get for doing a job: Mom gets her *pay* on Fridays.

peace /pēs/ *n.* **1** A condition without war. **2** Calmness: Let's have some *peace* and quiet.

peach /pēch/ *n., pl.* **peaches** A round fruit with a fuzzy, yellowish-pink skin and a large seed or pit.

pear /pâr/ *n.* A fruit with a green or yellowish-brown skin. A pear is round at the bottom and smaller near the stem.

pearl /pûrl/ *n.* A small, round white gem formed inside an oyster shell.

pen¹ /pen/ *n.* A writing tool that uses ink.

pen² /pen/ *n.* A small fenced area for animals: Put the pigs in the *pen*.

pen·cil /pen′səl/ *n.* A writing tool that has a stick of graphite inside wood.

pen·ny /pen′ē/ *n., pl.* **pennies** A coin worth one cent.

peo·ple /pe′pəl/ *n.* Plural of *person*.

per·haps /pər·haps′/ *adv.* Maybe; possibly: *Perhaps* I'll go with you.

per·son /pûr′sən/ *n., pl.* **people** or **persons** A human being.

pet /pet/ *n.* A tame animal kept in the house.

—*v.* **petted, petting** To stroke or pat: Our dog loves to be *petted*.

pick /pik/ *v.* **1** To choose: *Pick* the color you want. **2** To take or pull off with your fingers: I *picked* an apple off the tree.

pick·le /pik′əl/ *n.* A cucumber soaked in salt water or vinegar.

pic·ture /pik′chər/ *n.* **1** A painting, drawing, or photograph. **2** A movie.

piece /pēs/ *n.* **1** A part of a whole thing. **2** An amount of something: a *piece* of cheese.

pil·low /pil′ō/ *n.* A bag filled with feathers or other soft material: I rested my head on the *pillow*.

pi·lot /pī′lət/ *n.* The person who steers or guides an airplane.

pin /pin/ *n.* **1** A thin, pointed piece of wire used to fasten things together: The *pins* are in the sewing box. **2** A piece of jewelry fastened to a pin.

—*v.* **pinned, pinning** To fasten with a pin.

pi·rate /pī′rit/ *n.* A person who attacks and robs ships at sea.

pitch·er¹ /pich′ər/ *n.* A bottle with a spout for pouring.

pitch·er² /pich′ər/ *n.* A baseball player who throws the ball for the batter to hit.

place /plās/ *n.* **1** A certain space or area: Put an X in the right *place*. **2** A city, town, or other area: Elmwood is a nice *place* to live.

—*v.* **placed, placing** To put: *Place* your hands on your head.

plan /plan/ *n.* **1** An idea for doing or making something: We have a *plan* for earning money. **2** (*pl.*) Arrangements: vacation *plans*.

—v. **planned, planning** **1** To make a plan: *plan* a party. **2** To intend: We *plan* to visit Grandma.

plan·et /plan'it/ *n.* Any of the large bodies that move around the sun: Earth is a *planet*.

plant /plant/ *n.* A living thing that grows in soil or water.

—v. To put seeds or plants in the soil: We *planted* vegetables.

play·ground /plā'ground'/ *n.* An outside area for play.

plot /plot/ *n.* **1** A small piece of land: They will use that *plot* for a garden. **2** A secret plan. **3** The events in a story: That book has an exciting *plot*.

—v. **plotted, plotting** To plan something in secret.

pock·et /pok'it/ *n.* A small pouch sewn into clothing to hold money and other things.

point /point/ *n.* **1** The sharp end of something: The pencil has a sharp *point*. **2** A dot. **3** A unit in scoring: Our team has ten *points*.

—v. **1** To show or indicate: The teacher *pointed* out my mistakes. **2** To aim or direct.

po·lar /pō'lər/ *adj.* Having to do with the North or South Pole: *Polar* bears live in *polar* regions.

po·lice /pə·lēs'/ *n.* A group of people who work to keep order and make people obey the law.

po·lite /pə·līt'/ *adj.* Having good manners; not rude: It is *polite* to say "please."

po·ny /pō'nē/ *n., pl.* **ponies** A very small horse.

pop /pop/ *n.* A sudden sharp noise: The balloon broke with a loud *pop*.

—v. **popped, popping** To make or cause a sudden noise.

porch /pôrch/ *n., pl.* **porches** A covered opening to a house or building: the front *porch*.

prac·tice /prak'tis/ *v.* **practiced, practicing** To do something over and over so you can do it better.

—n. Doing something over and over to learn it better: Playing the piano well takes lots of *practice*.

pre·pare /pri·pâr'/ *v.* **prepared, preparing** To get or make ready: Dad is *preparing* dinner.

pre·tend /pri·tend'/ *v.* To make believe: Let's *pretend* that we are on a spaceship.

pret·ty /prit'ē/ *adj.* **prettier, prettiest** Attractive; pleasant.

price /prīs/ *n.* The amount of money something costs.

prin·cess /prin'sis/ *n.* The daughter of a king or queen.

print /print/ *n.* **1** Letters and words marked on paper with ink: This book has large *print*. **2** A mark made by pressing: Our feet left *prints* in the snow.

—v. **1** To put letters and words on paper: That machine *prints* newspapers. **2** To write letters as in print: *Print* your name here.

prize /prīz/ *n.* Something won in a contest or game.

prob·lem /prob'ləm/ *n.* Something to be solved: Rabbits in the garden are a *problem*. There were ten *problems* on the test.

---

act, āte, câre, ärt;   egg, ēven;   if, īce;   on, ōver, ôr;   book, food;   up, tûrn;
ə = a in *ago,* e in *listen,* i in *giraffe,* o in *pilot,* u in *circus;*   yoo = u in *music;*   oil;   out;
chair; sing; shop; thank; that; zh in *treasure.*

prom·ise /prom'is/ *n.* Words that show you will or you will not do something: I made a *promise.*
—*v.* **promised, promising** To give a promise.

prompt /prompt/ *adj.* Right on time: A *prompt* person is never late.

prop /prop/ *n.* Something that is used to hold something else up.
—*v.* **propped, propping** To hold something up with a prop: Paula *propped* up the plant with a stick.

proud /proud/ *adj.* Thinking well of: Sonia's parents are *proud* of her.

pud·ding /pood'ing/ *n.* A soft dessert made with milk and eggs.

pud·dle /pud'(ə)l/ *n.* A small pool of water: There were *puddles* in the street after the rain.

pull /pool/ *v.* **1** To draw something forward or toward yourself: The dogs *pulled* the sled. **2** To take or tear out: Dad is *pulling* weeds.

pump·kin /pump'kin *or* pung'kin/ *n.* A large, round orange fruit: Did you buy a Halloween *pumpkin?*

pup·py /pup'ē/ *n., pl.* **puppies** A very young dog.

pur·ple /pûr'pəl/ *n., adj.* A color that is a mixture of blue and red.

pur·pose /pûr'pəs/ *n.* A plan or aim: The *purpose* of this book is to teach spelling.

push /poosh/ *v.* To press against and move something: Polly *pushed* the chair under the table.
—*n.* The act of pushing: That *push* almost knocked Stan over.

puz·zle /puz'əl/ *n.* Something that is confusing or hard to do: Elsa likes to figure out *puzzles.*
—*v.* **puzzled, puzzling** To confuse: The secret message *puzzled* us.

Q

quick /kwik/ *adj.* Done in a short time; fast: a *quick* shower.

quite /kwīt/ *adv.* **1** Completely: I am *quite* happy now. **2** Really: Alvin lives *quite* near me.

R

rab·bit /rab'it/ *n.* A small animal with long ears and a fluffy tail.

rac·coon /ra·koon'/ *n.* A small, grayish-brown animal with a bushy tail. A raccoon has black marks on its face like a mask.

race¹ /rās/ *n.* A contest of speed: Iris won the swimming *race.*
—*v.* **raced, racing** **1** To take part in a race. **2** To move fast: I *raced* to the door.

race² /rās/ *n.* A group of people who are similar in the way they look.

rail·road /rāl'rōd'/ *n.* The track that trains move on.

rai·sin /rā'zən/ *n.* A dried grape.

ranch /ranch/ *n., pl.* **ranches** A large farm where cattle or horses are raised.

rath·er /rath'ər/ *adv.* **1** More willingly: I'd *rather* go tomorrow. **2** Instead: You should ask Philip *rather* than me.

reach /rēch/ *v.* **1** To touch or get hold of: Can you *reach* the top shelf? **2** To arrive at: He *reached* home before dark.

read /rēd/ *v.* **read** /red/, **reading** **1** To get meaning from letters and words. **2** To say aloud something that is written: Please *read* us a story.

re·al·ly /rē′lē *or* rē′ə·lē/ *adv.* **1** In fact: Did that *really* happen? **2** Very; truly: Grandpa was *really* happy to see us.

rea·son /rē′zən/ *n.* **1** Explanation; excuse: What *reason* do you have for being late? **2** Cause: Being sleepy is a *reason* for going to bed.

re·cess /rē′ses/ *n., pl.* **recesses** A short break from work: Let's play hopscotch during *recess.*

re·cite /ri·sīt′/ *v.* **recited, reciting** To repeat something learned by heart: Len can *recite* lots of poems.

reed /rēd/ *n.* The hollow stem of certain kinds of grass.

re·pair /ri·pâr′/ *v.* To fix or mend. —*n. (often pl.)* The act of repairing: Our car needs *repairs.*

re·turn /ri·tûrn′/ *v.* **1** To come or go back. **2** To give back: Ned *returned* his library book.

ride /rīd/ *v.* **rode, ridden, riding** **1** To sit on something and make it move: to *ride* a bike. **2** To be carried along: to *ride* on a bus. —*n.* **1** A trip made when riding. **2** Something such as a merry-go-round that you ride for fun.

right /rīt/ *adj.* **1** Good and just: the *right* thing to do. **2** Correct: the *right* answer. **3** The opposite of left: your *right* hand.

—*adv.* **1** According to what is good and just: You did *right* to tell him. **2** Correctly: Ed spelled the word *right.* **3** To the right: Turn *right.* **4** Exactly: Put the books *right* here. **5** With no delay: Go *right* to bed.

rise /rīz/ *v.* **rose, risen, rising** **1** To stand or get up. **2** To move higher: The sun *rises* in the east.

riv·er /riv′ər/ *n.* A large stream of water.

rob·in /rob′in/ *n.* A bird with a reddish-orange breast.

rock[1] /rok/ *n.* A stone; something that is very hard.

rock[2] /rok/ *v.* To move back and forth: I *rocked* the baby to sleep.

rode /rōd/ *v.* Past tense of *ride.*

roll /rōl/ *v.* **1** To turn over and over: The stone *rolled* down the hill. **2** To move on wheels: The wagon *rolled* down the street. —*n.* **1** Something wrapped around itself: a *roll* of paper towels. **2** A small loaf of bread.

roof /roof/ *n.* The top of a building.

room /room/ *n.* **1** Space: There's *room* for five people in the car. **2** An area within a house separated off by walls.

rose[1] /rōz/ *n.* A sweet-smelling flower that has thorns on its stem.

rose[2] /rōz/ *v.* Past tense of *rise.*

rough /ruf/ *adj.* **1** Not smooth; uneven: A cat's tongue feels *rough.* **2** Not gentle; rugged: Football can be a *rough* game. —*adv.* Not gently or carefully: Don't play *rough.*

---

act, āte, câre, ärt;   egg, ēven;   if, īce;   on, ōver, ôr;   book, food;   up, tûrn;
ə = a in *ago*, e in *listen*, i in *giraffe*, o in *pilot*, u in *circus;*   yoo = u in *music;*   oil;   out;
chair; si**ng**; **sh**op; **th**ank; **th**at; **zh** in *treasure.*

round /round/ *adj.* Having a shape like a circle or ball.

—*adv., prep.* **1** To move in a circle: The wheels turned *round*. **2** On all sides; around: The children sat *round* the teacher.

—*v.* To make round: We *rounded* the corners of the paper.

row¹ /rō/ *v.* To move a boat in water using oars.

row² /rō/ *n.* A line of things or people: We all stood in a *row*.

rub /rub/ *v.* **rubbed, rubbing** To press and move one thing against another: *Rub* the cat's back.

s

safe /sāf/ *adj.* **1** Free from danger or harm: Find a *safe* place to hide. **2** Not hurt: Sal was *safe*. **3** Careful: Mrs. Lopez is a *safe* driver.

—*n.* A metal box for keeping money and valuable things.

sail /sāl/ *n.* A piece of strong cloth that catches wind to move a boat.

—*v.* **1** To move on water or in air: The boat *sailed* into the bay. **2** To travel in a boat. **3** To run a sailboat: Brad is learning to *sail*.

sale /sāl/ *n.* **1** The act of selling: The clerk rang up the *sale*. **2** Selling things at low prices: The store is having a *sale* on boots.

same /sām/ *adj., pron.* Alike: Tammi and I bought the *same* ice cream.

sand·wich /sand′wich *or* san′wich/ *n., pl.* **sandwiches** Two slices of bread with food between them.

Sat. Abbreviation for *Saturday*.

Sat·ur·day /sat′ər·dē *or* sat′ər·dā/ *n.* The seventh day of the week.

save /sāv/ *v.* **saved, saving** **1** To take away from danger: The brave woman *saved* the child. **2** To keep money for a later time: Danny is *saving* for a bike. **3** To avoid waste: *Save* energy.

scent /sent/ *n.* A smell or odor: Flowers have a nice *scent*.

school /skool/ *n.* **1** A place where you learn. **2** The time when teaching is done: Let's play soccer after *school*.

scold /skōld/ *v.* To speak in an angry way: Dad *scolded* me for lying.

scratch /skrach/ *v.* **1** To mark with something sharp or rough: The cat *scratched* the table. **2** To scrape something that itches.

—*n., pl.* **scratches** A mark left by scratching.

scrub /skrub/ *v.* **scrubbed, scrubbing** To clean by rubbing very hard: *Scrub* the bathtub.

search /sûrch/ *v.* To look for or through: I'm *searching* for Nan.

—*n., pl.* **searches** The act of searching: We didn't find any shells during our *search*.

sec·ond¹ /sek′ənd/ *adj.* **1** Coming next after first. **2** Another: I'd like to buy a *second* toy.

—*adv.* In second place: Howie's team finished *second*.

sec·ond² /sek′ənd/ *n.* One of sixty parts of a minute in time.

se·cret /sē′krit/ *n.* Something you must not tell anyone else.
—*adj.* Known only to a few people: a *secret* meeting place.

see /sē/ *v.* **saw, seen, seeing** **1** What you do with your eyes. **2** To understand: I *see* what you mean. **3** To find out: *See* what he's doing.

seed /sēd/ *n.* The tiny thing from which a plant or tree grows.

seen /sēn/ *v.* Past participle of *see.*

sel·dom /sel′dəm/ *adv.* Not very often: Darrell is *seldom* late.

sell /sel/ *v.* **sold, selling** To give something in return for money: Mr. Roberts *sold* his car for $2,000.

send /send/ *v.* **sent, sending** To cause to go: We *sent* the dog home.

sent /sent/ *v.* Past tense and past participle of *send.*

sen·tence /sen′təns/ *n.* A group of words that makes sense by itself.

sev·enth /sev′ənth/ *adj.* Next after sixth.

shack /shak/ *n.* A small building, usually one in bad condition.

shad·ow /shad′ō/ *n.* The dark image made when a person or thing blocks the light.

shake /shāk/ *v.* **shook, shaken, shaking** **1** To move something back and forth or up and down quickly: *Shake* your head. **2** To tremble: Gerry *shook* with fear.

shall /shal/ *v.* A word used with other verbs to talk about the future: What *shall* I do next?

sham·poo /sham·pōō′/ *n.* A soap used to wash hair.
—*v.* To wash hair.

shape /shāp/ *n.* **1** The form of something: The *shape* of a ball is round. **2** The condition of someone or something: He is in good *shape.*
—*v.* **shaped, shaping** To give form to something: I *shaped* the clay into a ball.

she /shē/ *pron.* A word used in place of a girl's or woman's name.

shell /shel/ *n.* A hard outside covering: Turtles have *shells.*

she's /shēz/ She is.

shine /shīn/ *n.* Brightness.
—*v.* **shined, shone, shining** **1** To give off light: The stars *shine* at night. **2** To polish or make bright: *Shine* your shoes.

shook /shŏŏk/ *v.* Past tense of *shake.*

shop /shop/ *v.* **shopped, shopping** To look for things and buy them.
—*n.* A place where things are sold.

short /shôrt/ *adj.* **1** Not long: a *short* time. **2** Not tall. **3** Not enough: You are a nickel *short.*
—*n., pl.* **shorts** Pants that come above the knees.

should /shŏŏd/ *v.* Past tense of *shall.* Ought to: You *should* go home.

---

act, āte, câre, ärt; egg, ēven; if, īce; on, ōver, ôr; bŏŏk, fōōd; up, tûrn;
ə = a in *ago,* e in *listen,* i in *giraffe,* o in *pilot,* u in *circus;* yōō = u in *music;* oil; out;
chair; sing; shop; thank; that; zh in *treasure.*

shoul·der /shōl′dər/ *n.* The part of your body where your arm joins your body.

shout /shout/ *n.* A sudden loud yell: They heard a *shout* for help.
—*v.* **1** To make a sudden loud yell. **2** To talk loud.

shov·el /shuv′əl/ *n.* A tool used for digging.
—*v.* To use a shovel: Bonnie *shoveled* the snow.

shut /shut/ *v.* **shut, shutting** **1** To close: *Shut* the door. **2** To turn off: *Shut* off the light.

shy /shī/ *adj.* Quiet; not at ease with strangers: The *shy* boy was afraid to ask for help.

sick /sik/ *adj.* **1** Having an illness. **2** Tired of something: Oliver is *sick* of playing the same games.

sight /sīt/ *n.* **1** The act of seeing: The *sight* of home made him smile. **2** The ability to see. **3** What is seen: The sunset is a beautiful *sight*. **4** View; area reached by sight: out of *sight*.

sil·ver /sil′vər/ *n.* A shiny whitish-gray metal.
—*adj.* **1** Made of silver: a *silver* ring. **2** Having the color of silver.

since /sins/ *prep., adv., conj.* From then until now: Ruta has been here *since* Monday. I have seen her every day *since*. We have had fun *since* she came.

sing /sing/ *v.* **sang, sung, singing** To make music with your voice.

sir /sûr/ *n.* A title of respect used for a man.

sis·ter /sis′tər/ *n.* A girl who has the same parents as you do.

sit /sit/ *v.* **sat, sitting** To take a seat: Maury *sat* on the floor.

six /siks/ *n., adj.* The word for 6.

sixth /siksth/ *adj.* Next after fifth.

six·ty /siks′tē/ *n., adj.* The word for 60.

skate /skāt/ *n.* A boot or shoe with a metal blade or four small wheels attached to the bottom.
—*v.* **skated, skating** To move on skates: We *skate* in the park.

skin /skin/ *n.* The outside covering of people, animals, fruits, and vegetables.
—*v.* **skinned, skinning** To scrape off skin: Larry *skinned* his knee.

skirt /skûrt/ *n.* A piece of clothing that hangs from the waist.

sky /skī/ *n., pl.* **skies** The air above Earth: Planes fly in the *sky*.

slope /slōp/ *v.* **sloped, sloping** To be at an angle: That roof *slopes* down almost to the ground.
—*n.* A hillside: The children went down the *slope* on their sleds.

slow /slō/ *adj.* Not fast.
—*v.* To make or become slower: The car *slowed* down.
—*adv.* In a slow or careful way: Cars should go *slow* near schools.

small /smôl/ *adj.* Little; not large.

smash /smash/ *v.* **1** To break into pieces. **2** To crash into.

smell /smel/ *v.* **1** To get the scent of something through your nose: *Smell* the flowers. **2** To give off a scent: Garbage *smells* awful.
—*n.* **1** The sense used to recognize odors: Dogs have a good sense of *smell*. **2** An odor.

smile /smīl/ *v.* **smiled, smiling** To raise the corners of your mouth to show that you are happy.
—*n.* The act of smiling: Mrs. Gregor gave us a friendly *smile*.

smoke /smōk/ *n.* The dusty cloud that rises from anything burning.
—*v.* **smoked, smoking** To give off smoke: The fire *smoked*.

smooth /smooth/ *adj.* Without bumps or lumps: New sidewalk is smooth.
—*v.* To make something smooth.

snail /snāl/ *n.* A slow-moving animal with a shell on its back.

snake /snāk/ *n.* A reptile with no legs that moves by crawling.

sneeze /snēz/ *v.* **sneezed, sneezing** To blow air out through your nose and mouth: Dust makes me *sneeze*.
—*n.* The act of sneezing: A *sneeze* can be a sign of a cold.

snow /snō/ *n.* Small white flakes of frozen water.
—*v.* To fall as snow: Does it *snow* here in the winter?

soft /sôft/ *adj.* **1** Not hard. **2** Quiet; not loud: a *soft* voice.

sold /sōld/ *v.* Past tense and past participle of *sell*.

some·one /sum'wun'/ *pron.* Some person.

some·times /sum'tīmz'/ *adv.* Now and then: *Sometimes* we eat out.

son /sun/ *n.* What a boy or man is to his parents.

soon /soon/ *adv.* **1** In a little while.

2 Quickly: We'll be there as *soon* as we can.

sound /sound/ *n.* Anything that can be heard: Don't make a *sound*!
—*v.* **1** To make a sound: *Sound* the horn. **2** To seem: It *sounds* right to me.

soup /soop/ *n.* A liquid food made with water or milk, meat or fish, and vegetables.

south /south/ *n., adj., adv.* A direction; the opposite of north.

south·ern /suth'ərn/ *adj.* **1** Of or from the south. **2** Toward the south: the *southern* part of the state.

space /spās/ *n.* **1** The unlimited area that holds the universe: The rocket traveled through *space*. **2** A limited area: a parking *space*.

speak /spēk/ *v.* **spoke, spoken, speaking** **1** To say words; to talk. **2** To make a speech: Our teacher *spoke* at the meeting.

spell[1] /spel/ *v.* **1** To say or write the letters of a word. **2** To stand for sounds: C-a-r *spells* car.

spell[2] /spel/ *n.* Words that are supposed to have magic power: The wizard cast a *spell* on me.

spi·der /spī'dər/ *n.* An insect that has eight legs and spins a web.

spill /spil/ *v.* **1** To let fall or run out: Lenny *spilled* his milk. **2** To fall or flow: Water *spilled* on the floor.

split /split/ *v.* **split, splitting** **1** To cut lengthwise: We *split* logs for the fire. **2** To share: Let's *split* an order of french fries.

---

act, āte, câre, ärt;   egg, ēven;   if, īce;   on, ōver, ôr;   book, food;   up, tûrn;
ə = a in *ago*, e in *listen*, i in *giraffe*, o in *pilot*, u in *circus*;   yoo = u in *music*;   oil;   out;
chair; sing; shop; thank; that; zh in *treasure*.

spoil /spoil/ *v.* **1** To ruin: The rain *spoiled* our day at the beach. **2** To become bad: Milk *spoils* if it is not kept cold. **3** To give someone everything he or she wants: Grandma *spoils* the baby.

spoke[1] /spōk/ *v.* Past tense of *speak*.

spoke[2] /spōk/ *n.* Part of a wheel.

spot /spot/ *n.* **1** A mark or stain: A leopard has *spots*. **2** A place: The park is my favorite *spot*.
—*v.* **spotted, spotting** To notice: Ann *spotted* a deer in the woods.

spray /sprā/ *n.* Water or other liquid in fine drops: Mom uses hair *spray*.
—*v.* To send out liquid in fine drops: *Spray* water on the plants.

spread /spred/ *v.* **spread, spreading** **1** To open completely: The bird *spread* its wings. **2** To smooth on: Zelda *spread* jelly on her toast.

spring /spring/ *v.* **sprang** *or* **sprung, springing** To leap suddenly: The dog *sprang* at me.
—*n.* **1** The season after winter. **2** A flow of water out of the ground.

spy /spī/ *n., pl.* **spies** A person who watches other people secretly.
—*v.* **spied, spying** **1** To keep watch secretly: They *spied* on our club meeting. **2** To catch sight of: I *spied* Morgan in the corner.

stair /stâr/ *n.* A step that goes from one level to another: Jack ran up the *stairs*.

stalk /stôk/ *n.* A stem of a plant.

stam·mer /stam′ər/ *v.* To pause while you are talking or repeat sounds without wanting to: When she is nervous, Hilary *stammers*.

stamp /stamp/ *n.* **1** A small piece of paper with glue on the back: Put a *stamp* on the letter. **2** A tool that makes a mark: a rubber *stamp*.
—*v.* **1** To put your foot down hard: The angry boy *stamped* his foot. **2** To mark with a stamp.

stand /stand/ *v.* **stood, standing** **1** To take or keep an upright position. **2** To put up with: I can't *stand* the smell of paint.

star /stär/ *n.* **1** A shining body that appears in the sky at night. **2** A shape with five or six points: ☆ ☆ **3** An actor or actress who plays the main part.
—*v.* **starred, starring** To play the main part.

stare /stâr/ *v.* **stared, staring** To look hard, often without blinking: The dog *stared* at the cat.
—*n.* A long, hard look.

start /stärt/ *v.* **1** To begin. **2** To turn on: Dad *started* the car.

state /stāt/ *n.* **1** The way something is: The dogs were in an excited *state*. **2** An area within a country: There are fifty *states* in the United States.

stay /stā/ *v.* To remain: You can *stay* for one more hour.

step /step/ *n.* **1** A movement made by lifting your foot and putting it down in another place. **2** A stair: We sat on the front *steps*.

—*v.* **stepped, stepping** **1** To move by taking steps: Please *step* over here. **2** To put your foot down on: Don't *step* on the bug.

stew /st(y)o͞o/ *n.* A thick soup made with meat and vegetables.

stick[1] /stik/ *n.* A thin piece of wood.

stick[2] /stik/ *v.* **stuck, sticking** **1** To prick with something sharp: I *stuck* myself with a needle. **2** To fasten with glue or paste. **3** To put: I *stuck* the book in my desk.

still /stil/ *adj.* Quiet: The house is *still* because everyone is asleep.
—*adv.* **1** Not moving: Sit *still* during dinner. **2** To this time: Aaron is *still* sick.

stir /stûr/ *v.* **stirred, stirring** To mix.

stone /stōn/ *n.* A small piece of rock.

stood /sto͝od/ *v.* Past tense and past participle of *stand.*

stop /stop/ *v.* **stopped, stopping** **1** To come or bring to a halt: The cars *stopped* at the light. **2** To leave off doing something: *Stop* talking to Sara. **3** To keep from doing something: I *stopped* Tamara from leaving.
—*n.* **1** The act of stopping: The plane makes a *stop* in Denver. **2** The place where something stops: a bus *stop.*

sto·ry[1] /stôr′ē/ *n., pl.* **stories** **1** An account that tells what happened. **2** A tale: Harvey loves adventure *stories.*

sto·ry[2] /stôr′ē/ *n. pl.* **stories** A floor in a building or house.

stove /stōv/ *n.* Something used for cooking or heating.

strange /strānj/ *adj.* **1** Odd; unusual: You look *strange* in that costume. **2** Not known: There is a *strange* dog in our yard.

strap /strap/ *n.* A thin piece of leather or cloth used to close or hold something.

straw /strô/ *n.* **1** Dried grass or stalks: We put *straw* in the stalls for the horses. **2** A thin tube used for sucking up a drink.

street /strēt/ *n.* A road.

strike /strīk/ *v.* **struck, striking** **1** To hit: The car *struck* a tree. **2** To tell time by sounding a bell: The clock *struck* one.
—*n.* In baseball, a swing that misses the ball.

string /string/ *n.* A thin rope or cord: Rudy tied the box with *string.*
—*v.* **strung, stringing** To put on a string: It's fun to *string* beads.

stroll /strōl/ *v.* To walk in a slow, easy way.
—*n.* A slow walk: Caroline took a *stroll* in the park.

strong /strông/ *adj.* **1** Powerful; not weak: It takes a *strong* person to lift a heavy box. **2** Not easily broken: This rope is *strong.*

struck /struk/ *v.* Past tense and past participle of *strike.*

stud·y /stud′ē/ *v.* **studied, studying** To work to learn something.

stuff /stuf/ *n.* Lots of different things: Put this *stuff* away.
—*v.* To pack in; to fill: Annie *stuffed* the bag with presents.

sud·den /sud′(ə)n/ *adj.* Quick; without warning: a *sudden* stop.

---

act, āte, câre, ärt;   egg, ēven;   if, īce;   on, ōver, ôr;   bo͝ok, fo͞od;   up, tûrn;
ə = a in *ago,* e in *listen,* i in *giraffe,* o in *pilot,* u in *circus;*   yo͞o = u in *music;*   oil;   out;
ch**air**; si**ng**; **sh**op; **th**ank; **th**at; **zh** in *treasure.*

sug·ar /shŏŏg′ər/ *n.* Something used to make food sweet.

suit /sōōt/ *n.* A set of clothes made up of a jacket and pants or a jacket and skirt.

—*v.* To be right for: Let's meet at a time that *suits* everyone.

sum·mer /sum′ər/ *n.* The season that comes after spring.

Sun. Abbreviation for *Sunday.*

Sun·day /sun′dē *or* sun′dā/ *n.* The first day of the week.

sun·ny /sun′ē/ *adj.* **sunnier, sunniest** Filled with sunshine; bright: It was a *sunny* afternoon.

sun·rise /sun′rīz′/ *n.* The time when the sun rises.

sun·set /sun′set′/ *n.* The time when the sun goes down.

sup·ply /sə·plī′/ *v.* **supplied, supplying** To give what is needed: Dad *supplied* the money.

—*n., pl.* **supplies** Things that are needed to do something: Notebooks and pencils are school *supplies.*

sup·pose /sə·pōz′/ *v.* **supposed, supposing** To think or believe: I *suppose* I can go.

sur·prise /sə(r)·prīz′/ *v.* **surprised, surprising** To do something unexpected: Jo's parents *surprised* her with a puppy.

—*n.* **1** The feeling caused by something unexpected: We all giggled with *surprise.* **2** Something not expected: Mom had a *surprise* for me when I got home.

swal·low /swol′ō/ *v.* To make food or drink go from your mouth into your stomach.

swap /swop/ *v.* **swapped, swapping** To trade or exchange: Clyde *swapped* his yo-yo for a whistle.

swift /swift/ *adj.* Quick; fast: A deer is a *swift* animal.

swim /swim/ *v.* **swam, swimming** To use your arms and legs to move along in water.

T

ta·ble /tā′bəl/ *n.* **1** A piece of furniture that has a flat top and is held up by legs. **2** A list or chart: a *table* of numbers.

tag¹ /tag/ *n.* A small piece of paper or cloth: a price *tag.*

—*v.* **tagged, tagging** To follow closely: Her brother *tagged* along.

tag² /tag/ *n.* A game in which you chase and try to touch others.

—*v.* **tagged, tagging** To touch someone with your hand.

take /tāk/ *v.* **took, taken, taking 1** To get hold of: *Take* my hand. **2** To use: I *take* the bus to school. **3** To bring: We *took* the clock to the repair shop. **4** To receive: Jon *took* the message.

talk /tôk/ *v.* To say words.

—*n.* A conversation: Dad and I had a *talk* about airplanes.

tall /tôl/ *adj.* The opposite of short: Are you *tall* enough to reach the top shelf?

tap /tap/ *v.* **tapped, tapping** To hit or touch lightly: Lonnie *tapped* his pencil on the desk.

—*n.* A light touch: Ethan felt a *tap* on his shoulder.

tape /tāp/ *n.* **1** A long, narrow strip with one sticky side. **2** A plastic strip used to record sounds.

—*v.* **taped, taping 1** To put tape on something. **2** To record on tape: We *taped* the school concert.

taste /tāst/ *v.* **tasted, tasting** **1** To get the flavor of something: The cook *tasted* the soup. **2** To have a flavor: The soup *tasted* salty.

—*n.* The flavor of something: Sugar has a sweet *taste*.

taught /tôt/ *v.* Past tense and past participle of *teach*.

teach /tēch/ *v.* **taught, teaching** To help someone learn.

teach·er /tē′chər/ *n.* A person who helps others learn.

team /tēm/ *n.* **1** A group of people who work or play together: Our baseball *team* won the game. **2** Animals that do work together.

ten /ten/ *n., adj.* The word for *10*.

tenth /tenth/ *adj.* Next after ninth.

test /test/ *n.* A way to find out how much someone has learned.

—*v.* To give a test; to try out: I *tested* the watch to see if it worked.

that's /thats *or* thəts/ That is.

their /thâr/ *pron.* Belonging to them.

then /then/ *adv.* **1** At that time: I was only four *then*. **2** Next: Go to school and *then* come home.

—*n.* A certain time: Can you be here by *then*?

there /thâr/ *adv.* At or to that place: Let's go *there* for dinner.

there's /thârz/ There is.

they /thā/ *pron.* More than one person or thing: *They* are friends.

they're /thâr/ They are.

think /thingk/ *v.* **thought, thinking** **1** To use your mind to remember, imagine, or solve a problem. **2** To believe: I *think* you are right.

third /thûrd/ *adj.* Next after second.

thirst·y /thûrs′tē/ *adj.* Needing or wanting something to drink.

thir·teen /thûr′tēn′/ *n., adj.* The word for *13*.

thir·ty /thûr′tē/ *n., adj.* The word for *30*.

those /thōz/ *adj., pron.* Plural of *that;* the ones there: *Those* pencils are mine. These pencils are longer than *those*.

though /thō/ *conj.* In spite of the fact that: I like tennis, *though* I don't play it well.

—*adv.* However: Juan took the medicine. He didn't like it, *though*.

thought[1] /thôt/ *n.* An idea: Think happy *thoughts*.

thought[2] /thôt/ *v.* Past tense and past participle of *think*.

thou·sand /thou′zənd/ *adj., n.* The word for *1,000*.

three /thrē/ *n., adj.* The word for *3*.

throat /thrōt/ *n.* The back part of your mouth: a sore *throat*.

thumb /thum/ *n.* The short, thick finger on one side of your hand.

Thurs. Abbreviation for *Thursday*.

Thurs·day /thûrz′dē *or* thûrz′dā/ *n.* The fifth day of the week.

---

act, āte, câre, ärt;   egg, ēven;   if, īce;   on, ōver, ôr;   book, food;   up, tûrn;
ə = a in *ago*, e in *listen*, i in *giraffe*, o in *pilot*, u in *circus;*   yoo = u in *music;*   oil;   out;
chair;   sing;   shop;   thank;   that;   zh in *treasure*.

tick·le /tik′əl/ *v.* **tickled, tickling** To touch someone in a way that makes a person laugh.

ti·ger /tī′gər/ *n.* A large animal of the cat family. A tiger has a yellow body with black stripes.

time /tīm/ *n.* **1** What is measured by years, months, weeks, days, hours, and minutes. **2** A point in time: What *time* is it now? **3** Someone's experience: Kate had a good *time.* **4** The number of actions that are repeated: Kyle wrote the word five *times.*

tire¹ /tīr/ *n.* The rubber that goes around a wheel.

tire² /tīr/ *v.* **tired, tiring** To make or become weak or sleepy.

ti·tle /tīt′(ə)l/ *n.* The name of a book, a song, or something else.

to /tōō/ *prep.* **1** In the direction of: Les went *to* his room. **2** Until: We are at school from 9 *to* 3. **3** On: Tape the card *to* the box.

to·day /tə·dā′/ *n.* This day; the present time: *Today* is Friday. —*adv.* On this day: Susan worked hard *today.*

to·geth·er /tə·geth′ər/ *adv.* **1** With each other: The children played *together.* **2** Into one: Neila knotted the ropes *together.*

to·mor·row /tə·mor′ō *or* tə·môr′ō/ *n.* The day after today.

ton·sil /ton′səl/ *n.* One of two oval-shaped tissues in the throat: Marcia had her *tonsils* taken out.

too /tōō/ *adv.* **1** Also. **2** More than enough: It is *too* cold to swim.

took /tŏŏk/ *v.* Past tense of *take.*

tooth /tōōth/ *n., pl.* **teeth** **1** One of the hard white parts in your mouth used to bite and chew. **2** Anything like a tooth: The comb has a broken *tooth.*

top¹ /top/ *n.* **1** The highest part: Touch the *top* of your head. **2** A cover or lid: a bottle *top.* —*adj.* Highest; best: The book is on the *top* shelf. Vera is the *top* student in her class. —*v.* **topped, topping** **1** To put on top: I *topped* my cereal with fruit. **2** To do or be better: Hank's score *topped* mine.

top² /top/ *n.* A toy that spins.

to·tal /tōt′(ə)l/ *n.* The whole amount: Add the numbers to find the *total.* —*adj.* Complete: The story he told was a *total* lie. —*v.* To add: You must *total* the numbers to find the answer.

touch /tuch/ *v.* **1** To put your hand or another part of your body on or against something: Don't *touch* the hot stove. **2** To be up against: The sofa *touches* the wall.

tough /tuf/ *adj.* **1** Strong; rugged. **2** Hard to chew. **3** Hard to do: It's *tough* to get up early.

tour·ist /tŏŏr′ist/ *n.* A person who travels and visits other places.

tow·el /toul *or* tou′əl/ *n.* Cloth or paper used to dry something.

tow·er /tou′ər/ *n.* A tall, narrow building or part of a building.

town /toun/ *n.* A small city.

trail /trāl/ *n.* **1** A path. **2** The marks left by a person or animal.
—*v.* To follow behind: Jacob *trailed* everyone in the race.

train /trān/ *n.* A line of railroad cars.
—*v.* To teach: I *trained* my dog to roll over.

tramp /tramp/ *v.* **1** To walk with a heavy step: Mino *tramped* down the stairs. **2** To walk or wander: We *tramped* around in the woods.
—*n.* A person who wanders about and has no home.

trap /trap/ *n.* **1** A thing used to catch animals. **2** A trick to catch people off guard: The police set a *trap* for the robbers.
—*v.* **trapped, trapping** To catch and hold: Spider webs *trap* flies.

trav·el /trav′əl/ *v.* To go from one place to another: We *traveled* to Canada.

trick /trik/ *n.* **1** Something done to fool or cheat. **2** Something clever or skillful: magic *tricks*.
—*v.* To fool or cheat: They *tricked* Chet into thinking they had left.

trip /trip/ *n.* A journey or vacation.
—*v.* **tripped, tripping** To stumble or make fall: Andrea *tripped* over a rock. Hal stuck out his foot and *tripped* Anton.

trou·sers /trou′zərz/ *n., pl.* A pair of pants.

try /trī/ *v.* **tried, trying** **1** To make an effort. **2** To test: *Try* the soup to see if it needs salt.
—*n., pl.* **tries** A chance: You have three *tries* to hit the target.

Tues. Abbreviation for *Tuesday.*

Tues·day /t(y)ōōz′dē *or* t(y)ōōz′dā/ *n.* The third day of the week.

tun·nel /tun′əl/ *n.* A narrow way under a river or a mountain.

turn /tûrn/ *v.* **1** To move around: He *turned* over in his sleep. **2** To change direction: We *turned* right at the corner. **3** To change: The leaves *turned* brown.
—*n.* A time or chance: It's your *turn* to do the dishes.

tur·tle /tûr′təl/ *n.* A slow-moving animal with a hard shell.

twelve /twelv/ *n., adj.* The word for *12.*

twen·ty /twen′tē/ *n., adj.* The word for *20.*

two /tōō/ *n., adj.* The word for *2.*

U

un·cle /ung′kəl/ *n.* **1** Your mother's or father's brother. **2** Your aunt's husband.

un·less /un·les′/ *conj.* Except if: We won't go *unless* you go too.

un·til /un·til′/ *prep., conj.* Up to the time of or when: I slept *until* nine o'clock. We played outside *until* it got dark.

---

act, āte, câre, ärt;   egg, ēven;   if, īce;   on, ōver, ôr;   bŏŏk, fōōd;   up, tûrn;
ə = a in *ago,* e in *listen,* i in *giraffe,* o in *pilot,* u in *circus;*   yōō = u in *music;*   oil;   out;
chair; sing; shop; thank; that; zh in *treasure.*

use /yo͞oz/ *v.* **used, using** **1** To put into action. **2** To finish: Alex *used* up all the paint.

—*n.* /yo͞os/ **1** The act of using. **2** Reason: There is no *use* crying.

—**used to** **1** Familiar with: I'm *used to* getting up early. **2** Did in the past: Miro *used to* live here.

V

val·ley /val'ē/ *n.* A low area between mountains or hills.

vil·lage /vil'ij/ *n.* A small town.

voice /vois/ *n.* **1** The sound made through the mouth. **2** The ability to make sounds: Helene lost her *voice* and could not sing.

vote /vōt/ *n.* A formal choice.

—*v.* **voted, voting** To choose by a vote: Americans *vote* for President every four years.

W

wag /wag/ *v.* **wagged, wagging** To move quickly: Dogs *wag* their tails.

—*n.* A wagging motion: The dog knocked over the lamp with a *wag* of its tail.

walk /wôk/ *v.* **1** To go on foot. **2** To make to walk: *Walk* the dog. **3** To walk with: *Walk* me home.

—*n.* **1** The act of walking: We took a *walk*. **2** The distance walked: It is a long *walk* home.

want /wont *or* wônt/ *v.* To wish for: Sheila *wants* a new pair of skates.

wash /wôsh *or* wäsh/ *v.* To clean with soap and water.

—*n.* Clothing washed at one time: Elyse helped me fold the *wash*.

was·n't /wuz'ənt *or* woz'ənt/ Was not.

wave /wāv/ *v.* **waved, waving** **1** To flutter: The flags *waved* in the wind. **2** To move your hand to greet or to signal.

—*n.* **1** A moving ridge of water. **2** The act of waving your hand.

we /wē/ *pron.* I and others: *We* all went camping.

weak /wēk/ *adj.* Not having strength: A cold makes me *weak*.

weath·er /weth'ər/ *n.* The state of the air: warm *weather*.

Wed. Abbreviation for *Wednesday*.

Wednes·day /wenz'dē *or* wenz'dā/ *n.* The fourth day of the week.

week /wēk/ *n.* Seven days.

week·end /wēk'end'/ *n.* Saturday and Sunday.

week·ly /wēk'lē/ *adj., adv.* Once a week: I get a *weekly* allowance. The show is on TV *weekly*.

wel·come /wel'kəm/ *v.* **welcomed, welcoming** To greet gladly: Our dog *welcomed* us home.

—*n.* A friendly greeting: Aunt Katie gave me a warm *welcome*.

—*adj.* Freely allowed: You are *welcome* to borrow my book.

we'll /wēl/ **1** We will. **2** We shall.

we're /wir/ We are.

weren't /wûrnt *or* wûr'ənt/ Were not.

west /west/ *n., adj., adv.* A direction; where the sun goes down.

what's /(h)wots *or* (h)wuts/ What is.

wheel /(h)wēl/ *n.* A round thing that turns in a circle to move a car, wagon, bicycle, or similar thing.

wheth·er /(h)weth'ər/ *conj.* If: Let me know *whether* you will come or not.

which /(h)wich/ *adj., pron.* What one or ones of several: *Which* book did you read? *Which* do you like best?

whirl /(h)wûrl/ *v.* To spin or make to spin around very fast: The skaters *whirled* around on the ice.

who /hoo/ *pron.* **1** What person: *Who* is ready? **2** That: Anyone *who* came got a prize.

who·ev·er /hoo-ev'ər/ *pron.* Any person who: *Whoever* comes will have a good time.

whole /hōl/ *adj.* Complete; all of: The *whole* class got A's.
—*n.* The entire thing.

who's /hooz/ **1** Who is: *Who's* ready for recess? **2** Who has: *Who's* got my notebook?

whose /hooz/ *pron.* Belonging to which person: *Whose* book is this?

why /(h)wī/ *adv.* For what reason.

wide /wīd/ *adj.* **wider, widest** **1** Far from side to side: The puddle was too *wide* to jump across. **2** Having a distance from side to side: My desk is one meter *wide*.
—*adv.* All the way: *wide* open.

wild /wīld/ *adj.* **1** Living or growing in nature; not tame: a *wild* animal. **2** Crazy or unbelievable: a *wild* story.

will /wil/ *v.* **would** A word used with other verbs to tell what is going to happen or what can be: Our school *will* be closed tomorrow. The car *will* hold five people.

win /win/ *v.* **won, winning** To do better than all others: Peter *won* the race.

wind¹ /wind/ *n.* **1** Moving air: The *wind* blew my hat off. **2** Breath: I had the *wind* knocked out of me.

wind² /wīnd/ *v.* **wound, winding** **1** To wrap around: Sharon *wound* the yarn into a ball. **2** To make a machine go by turning a part of it: I forgot to *wind* my watch. **3** To turn and twist: The road *winds* through the mountains.

win·dow /win'dō/ *n.* An opening in a wall that lets in air and light.

wipe /wīp/ *v.* **wiped, wiping** To clean or dry by rubbing: Please *wipe* your feet on the mat.

wise /wīz/ *adj.* **wiser, wisest** Having or showing good sense: My parents gave me *wise* advice.

wish /wish/ *n., pl.* **wishes** A hope or desire: My *wish* came true.
—*v.* **1** To hope for something: Mara *wished* for a pony. **2** To make a wish: Have you ever *wished* on a star?

with·out /with-out' *or* with-out'/ *prep.* With no: Mother cooks *without* salt.

won /wun/ *v.* Past tense and past participle of *win*.

won·der /wun'dər/ *v.* To want to know: I *wonder* where he is.

won't /wōnt/ Will not.

wood /wood/ *n.* What makes up the trunk and branches of a tree.

---

act, āte, câre, ärt;   egg, ēven;   if, īce;   on, ōver, ôr;   book, food;   up, tûrn;
ə = a in *ago*, e in *listen*, i in *giraffe*, o in *pilot*, u in *circus*;   yoo = u in *music*;   oil;   out;
chair;   sing;   shop;   thank;   that;   zh in *treasure*.

wood·en /wо͝od′(ə)n/ *adj.* Made of wood: *wooden* toys.

wool /wо͝ol/ *n.* **1** The hair of sheep. **2** Yarn or cloth made from sheep's hair: My coat is made of *wool*.
—*adj.* Made of wool: a *wool* scarf.

word /wûrd/ *n.* **1** A sound or group of sounds that has meaning. **2** The letters that stand for a word.

work /wûrk/ *n.* **1** The effort needed to do something: Pulling weeds is hard *work*. **2** A job.
—*v.* **1** To make an effort: Doug *works* hard. **2** To have a job: Dad *works* for the newspaper. **3** To run: That radio does not *work*.

world /wûrld/ *n.* **1** Earth: Blake would like to travel around the *world*. **2** Everything; the universe.

wor·ry /wûr′ē/ *v.* **worried, worrying** To be or make someone uneasy or upset: Mom will *worry* if I don't go straight home.
—*n., pl.* **worries** Something that makes you worry.

worst /wûrst/ *adj.* Least good or well: I made the *worst* mistake of all.

worth /wûrth/ *prep.* **1** Good enough for: The zoo is a place *worth* visiting. **2** Having the same value: A dime is *worth* ten cents.
—*n.* Value: We got our money's *worth*.

would /wо͝od/ *v.* Past tense of *will*. *Would* is often used to talk about wants and to ask polite questions: I *would* like another sandwich. *Would* you help me?

wrap /rap/ *v.* **wrapped, wrapping** To put a cover around something: Theo *wrapped* the present.

wreck /rek/ *v.* To destroy: The storm *wrecked* our tree house.
—*n.* Something that has been ruined: That car is a *wreck*.

wren /ren/ *n.* A small songbird.

wrist /rist/ *n.* The place where your hand joins your arm.

write /rīt/ *v.* **wrote, written, writing** **1** To make letters and words. **2** To be an author: Diane is *writing* a book.

writ·ten /rit′(ə)n/ *v.* Past participle of *write*.

wrote /rōt/ *v.* Past tense of *write*.

Y

yard¹ /yärd/ *n.* The land around a building: the front *yard*.

yard² /yärd/ *n.* A measure equal to 3 feet or 36 inches.

yel·low /yel′ō/ *n., adj.* The color of a lemon.

yes·ter·day /yes′tər·dē *or* yes′tər·dā′/ *n.* The day before today.
—*adv.* On the day before today: There was no school *yesterday*.

your /yôr *or* yо͝or/ *pron.* Belonging to you: Is this *your* pencil?

you're /yо͝or *or* yôr/ You are.

your·self /yôr·self′ *or* yо͝or·self′/ *pron., pl.* **yourselves** Your own self: Help *yourself* to an apple.

Aa Bb Cc Dd

Ee Ff Gg Hh

Ii Jj Kk Ll

Mm Nn Oo

Pp Qq Rr Ss

Tt Uu Vv Ww

Xx Yy Zz

Aa Bb Cc Dd

Ee Ff Gg Hh

Ii Jj Kk Ll

Mm Nn Oo

Pp Qq Rr Ss

Tt Uu Vv Ww

Xx Yy Zz

D 5
E 6
F 7
G 8
H 9
I 10
J 1